'EVERYTHING ABOUT THIS BOO[K]
THE RECIPES, THE PHOTOGRA[PH]
LIFE – IS COMPLETELY BEGUILING. A DELIGHT.'

Mark D[...]

Niki Segnit

'A VERY APT BOOK ABOUT
THE MARTINI – IT IS CRISP,
ELEGANT AND DANGEROUSLY
SEDUCTIVE.'

*'Alice has fine taste and is always meticulously researched so
it makes me very happy to have her thoughts on vital matters
such as Martini proportions, garnishes and which gin in this
slim and perfect volume.'*

VICTORIA MOORE

the Martini

**THE ULTIMATE GUIDE
TO A COCKTAIL ICON**

by Alice Lascelles

FOR AILANA
WHO LOVED A MARTINI

MANAGING DIRECTOR: Sarah Lavelle

EDITOR: Sarah Thickett

SERIES DESIGNER: Maeve Bargman

DESIGNER: Katy Everett

PHOTOGRAPHER: Laura Edwards

COPY EDITOR: Nick Funnell

PROOFREADER: Emma Bastow

PRODUCTION CONTROLLER: Martina Georgieva

HEAD OF PRODUCTION: Stephen Lang

First published in 2024 by Quadrille Publishing Limited

Quadrille
52–54 Southwark Street
London SE1 1UN
quadrille.com

Cataloguing in Publication Data: a catalogue record for this book is available from the British Library.

ISBN: 978 1 83783 135 7

FSC
www.fsc.org

MIX
Paper | Supporting
responsible forestry
FSC® C018179

Printed in China

CONTENTS

INTRODUCTION

There is something particularly delightful about hearing the words:

'Shall we have a Martini?'

As soon as they're uttered, the ante is upped. There is a little charge of excitement. You and the asker are now in cahoots – and that's before you've even taken a sip…

The first Martini I ever had was a Vesper at the Dorchester.

I was in my early twenties and had just landed a job as a reporter on a drinks magazine, despite the fact that I knew absolutely nothing about drinks. As luck would have it, I ran into Robbie Bargh, a rather fabulous hospitality consultant who spent his days designing cocktail bars for some of the world's top hotels. Bargh was appalled by my mixological ignorance, so he whisked me off to the Dorchester (at some wholly inappropriate time like 3pm on a Monday afternoon, I recall), sat me down on a plush banquette and ordered me a Vesper.

I can still see that icy chalice now, sitting on its embossed coaster: the star-bright liquid, marbled with lemon oils, rising silkily to the rim; the Y-shaped glass, once frosted, gradually beading with condensation.

Robbie told me the recipe had been invented by *James Bond* author Ian Fleming. I took a sip, and then sat there, rapt, as its cold fire hit my solar plexus.

In the two decades since, my hunt for a good Martini has taken me all over the world: from the high-rise bars of Tokyo, to some of Brooklyn's crummiest dives; from the rain-lashed moors of Northumbria, to St James's fanciest hotels.

I've had Martinis in Delhi, Barcelona, Paris and Milan; and one very memorable Lychee Martini in a speakeasy hidden out the back of a Panamanian hair salon.

Surrounded by the world's best mixologists, I've sipped in memoriam Martinis by the grave of Savoy bartender Harry Craddock. We travelled there in a cavalcade of vintage cars and drank our toast from iced Thermoses.

I've clocked up thousands of miles in the name of vermouth and gin. And the reason I've done this is because the Martini is so much more than just a drink.

It's a platonic ideal, a totem – a sort of boozy cultural prism. A drink bound by recondite rules, and steeped in lore and superstition.

Its minutiae have had some of the world's greatest minds dancing on a pin – Ernest Hemingway, J. Robert Oppenheimer, Ian Fleming, Winston Churchill, Dorothy Parker, Homer Simpson.

It's the sum-total of all that's exquisite, yet it's also a kind of perfection that's well within one's grasp. You're just as likely to discover your dream Martini at your kitchen table as you are in a world-class bar. Because the way you take your Martini is as particular as the way you take your tea. Is there any other cocktail that requires the bartender to first ask you how *you* like it?

If you never mixed a Martini yourself you'd only know the half of it. Because all the little rituals involved in its preparation are a big part of its magic: choosing the gin, cracking the ice, cutting the scented twist. It's an antidote to a world of infernal distractions; a chance to be fully present.

The one thing nicer than mixing yourself a Martini is mixing one for somebody else. Getting it just how they like it – even if you don't really approve – is the ultimate act of kindness.

This book contains 60-odd recipes that help tell the Martini's story, from its origins in the late 1800s right through to the 21st century. Some hinge on almost laughably tiny tweaks while others are so complex they're almost culinary. (I'm sure a few will have some of you throwing the book at the wall and shouting 'That is JUST NOT A MARTINI!')

If you don't know what your perfect Martini looks like, I hope this book may help you find it. And if you *do*, perhaps some of the tips and tricks herein will help you improve it.

Because it's a drink that journeys with you – not a recipe that's fixed. It's an icon that you can make truly your own. And *that* is why it's a classic.

AL

THE MARTINI THEN AND NOW

The Martini's origins are woozy – no one knows exactly when it was created, or by whom. But it was probably born in a smoke-filled New York club or saloon some time in the 1880s – a point in time that produced many of the most enduring recipes and cocktail books.

Vermouth, still relatively new to the States at this point, was the aperitif du jour, and its popularity inspired many riffs on the spirit-and-vermouth formula: the Manhattan (which is really just a Martini made with sweet, instead of dry, vermouth and whisky instead of gin); the more baroque Turf Cocktail (*p.107*), and the Martinez (*p.96*), a mix of sweet Old Tom gin, red vermouth and bitters that's a sort of halfway-house between a Martini and a Manhattan.

There was also a cocktail around this time variously known as the Martini, Martineau, Martigny or Martine, which was made with sweet Old Tom, red or 'Italian' vermouth, bitters, orange curaçao and an olive. A Martini by name, perhaps, but not yet a Martini as we might think of it.

Cocktails in this era were generally sweet. But as distilling improved and London Dry gin caught on, drinkers' palates evolved. And by the turn of the 20th century dry cocktails had became the sophisticate's bar call.

'When a customer comes in and orders a sweet drink… I know at once that he's from the country,' said a bar owner to the *New York Herald* in 1897. 'In all my acquaintance with city men, I know not more than half a dozen who can stand drinking sweet things. […] They want everything dry, the drier, the better.' (Taken from *Imbibe!* by David Wondrich)

The new-look Martini was made with London Dry gin, dry (or 'French') vermouth and a dash of orange bitters. It was dry by the standards of the time, but it was still mixed pretty wet: two parts gin to one part vermouth, or even 50/50.

THE BIRTH OF THE COCKTAIL HOUR

Before Prohibition, cocktail drinking was largely done in public, in gentlemen's clubs and saloons; the introduction of the Volstead Act in 1920 drove it into people's homes. The Great Depression, which followed soon after, forced many American households to lay off staff. And the result of all this was that hosts increasingly had to mix the drinks themselves.

Sales of domestic cocktail kits duly went through the roof and silver companies including Asprey, Tiffany and Dunhill responded by launching playful art deco designs in the shape of aeroplanes, skyscrapers, battleships and penguins.

The cocktail hour became a ritual as performative as carving the turkey; and the Martini its sacrament, fetishised right down to the very last detail.

Quite why it became de rigueur to use ever-decreasing amounts of vermouth is not entirely clear – one theory is it was simply an attempt to make a virtue of war-time shortages. But a whole industry sprang up peddling accessories for micro-dosing vermouth: atomisers, droppers, finely calibrated Martini 'scales' and vermouth-soaked Martini 'stones'.

There are apocryphal tales of Winston Churchill bowing in the direction of France as a substitute for Noilly Prat, and people whispering 'vermouth' down the phone, or simply allowing a beam of sun to shine through a bottle of vermouth onto a glass of gin. There are even stories of bars charging more the less vermouth a Martini contained.

The bone-dry Martini became a signifier of intellect; a show of political strength. In 1943, President Roosevelt mixed one of his (reputedly rather poor) Martinis for Stalin. The Russian dictator pronounced it 'cold on the stomach'.

The Martini's macho reputation was cemented by *James Bond* author Ian Fleming, when he chose, in the fifties, to make it the cocktail of choice of his hard-drinking secret agent (**see** *Vesper p.83*).

The Martini figured in movies, literature, art and design (Lowell Edmunds' *Martini, Straight Up* gives a very scholarly account of its cultural symbolism). It was so central to life in Hollywood it even spawned its own film-making slang: the 'Martini Shot' or 'Martini' is jargon for the final shot set-up of the day.

The 1960s and 70s were the decades that gave the world the 'Three-Martini Lunch' – a liquid repast that was classed as fully tax-deductible on the basis that it stoked the creativity of Madison Avenue's advertising executives (the so-called 'Mad Men').

The Martini went on getting drier, until it terminated in the See-Thru (*p.95*) – a glass of gin (or vodka) served without a single drop of vermouth.

There was only one way for the pendulum swing, and that was back the other way. And in the 1980s the word 'Martini' was hijacked for pretty much any cocktail served in a glass that was Y-shaped.

These 'alterna-tinis' were adulterated with fruit juice, coffee liqueur and blue curaçao. The reign of the Puritan Dry Martini was well and truly over.

But with the dawn of the new millennium came a revival in vintage drinks – one that coincided, most fortuitously, with a worldwide boom in gin distilling and a vermouth renaissance.

And today, more than a decade later, the party rages on – the Martini is as popular as it's ever been. But it's evolved into a hi-lo drink that cuts across the spectrum – equally at home in a five-star hotel, a dive bar or a domestic kitchen.

And while the reverence for the canonical recipes remains, that mid-century dogmatism is gone – the 21st century Martini is more enquiring and cosmopolitan.

Bartenders have used techniques gleaned from chefs and perfumers to imbue the Martini with a whole new palette of flavours – flint, shiso, lichen, seaweed, pandan leaves, olive oil and oyster shells.

And it's that capacity for reinvention that makes the Martini a resolutely modern drink. It's not just an exercise in nostalgia – unless, of course, you want it to be.

How did the Martini get its name? Historians can't agree. Some say it was named for the Martini-Henry rifle; others, for a cocktail-loving judge called Randolph B. Martine. But it's most likely it simply became synonymous with a famous brand of vermouth people often mixed it with.

**'HE WAS WHITE AND SHAKEN,
LIKE A DRY MARTINI.'**

'I LOVE TO DRINK MARTINIS,

TWO AT THE VERY MOST

THREE, I'M UNDER THE TABLE

FOUR, I'M UNDER THE HOST.'

'BECAUSE ALL MY LIFE I'VE BEEN TERRIBLE AT REMEMBERING
PEOPLE'S NAMES. ONCE I INTRODUCED A FRIEND OF MINE
AS 'MARTINI'. HER NAME WAS ACTUALLY 'OLIVE'.'

Actress Tallulah Bankhead on why she called everyone 'darling'

**'COULD ANY TIGER
DRINK MARTINIS, SMOKE CIGARS,
AND LAST AS WE DO?'**

WH Auden, Symmetries & Asymmetries (1965)

'A MANHATTAN YOU SHAKE TO FOX-TROT TIME,
A BRONX TO TWO-STEP TIME, A DRY MARTINI
YOU ALWAYS SHAKE TO WALTZ TIME.'

William Powell in The Thin Man (1934)

'HE KNOWS JUST HOW
I LIKE MY MARTINI:
FULL OF ALCOHOL.'

*Homer Simpson,
The Simpsons (2010)*

*Charles Butterworth in
Every Day's a Holiday (1937)*

'YOU OUGHT TO GET OUT
OF THOSE WET CLOTHES
AND INTO A DRY MARTINI.'

Jared Brown

'A DRY
MARTINI
IS A MIXED
BLESSING'

HL Mencken

'MARTINIS ARE THE ONLY
AMERICAN INVENTION AS
PERFECT AS THE SONNET.'

FATIMA BLUSH: I MADE YOU ALL WET.
JAMES BOND: YES, BUT MY MARTINI IS STILL DRY.

Never Say Never Again (1983)

INGREDIENTS

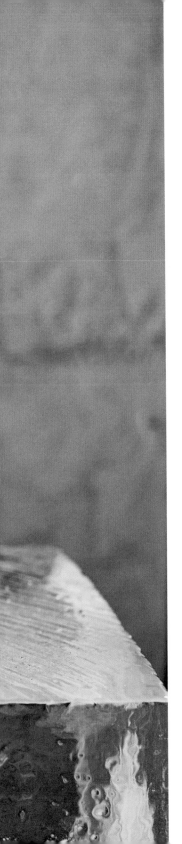

ICE

A warm Martini is a lousy Martini, however well it's mixed. So consider ice (and coldness in general) your number one ingredient.

Ice is important because it chills the cocktail, which makes it exciting to touch and taste. It gives it energy and definition, but also cools its alcoholic strength. It adds an all-important drop of dilution, which helps the botanicals to breath. And it makes the drink look nice – is there any sight more tantalising than a freshly iced Martini?

The more ice you use, the slower it melts, which gives you more control over the rate of dilution – so always fill your shaker or mixing glass at least two-thirds full of cubes. Big cubes melt slower than small ones, as they have a lower surface area to volume ratio. So if you have the choice, chunkier cubes are the way to go.

The best tray I've found for regular ice is the £10 Bar Original Silicone Ice Tray. It's flexible, stackable, easy to turn out and makes 32 good-sized cubes. I keep two on rotation in my freezer at all times, so at least one is always full.

I also like to have a stash of extra-large hunks or cubes for slow-sipping drinks that are served over ice, like the Martini on the Rocks. There are lots of companies that sell silicone moulds that do cubes that will fill a whole glass. But I prefer to just freeze a big ice block in a plastic container and hack it to bits – the jagged bergs you get are all the more beautiful, I think, for their irregularity.

(To stop the ice block sliding around when you hack it up, place it on a tea towel first. And then store the chunks in the freezer in a box or resealable bag.)

Boiling or purifying the water first may make your ice taste nicer, but it won't make it clearer, I'm afraid, because the cause of cloudiness in ice is usually air bubbles rather than impurities. It is possible to make crystal clear ice at home using a method called 'directional freezing' – it's a bit of a faff, but if you want to give it a try *The Ice Book* by Camper English is the last word on all things icy.

For a really special occasion you could get some beautiful ice delivered to your door – Ice Studio in London does stunning blocks, bars and spheres clear enough to read a book through.

Store ice well away from the bolognese and fish fingers, ideally in a box, bag or separate drawer, so it doesn't acquire nasty smells. And always, *always* refill your ice tray before returning it to the freezer.

SUPER-COLD MARTINIS

Can a Martini ever be too cold? Yes, if it's frozen solid. But you've got to go pretty sub-zero before this becomes a problem.

A spirit that's 40% alcohol by volume will freeze at around -27°C – well below the temperature of a domestic freezer, which is usually around -18°C.

A mixed Martini, however, has a lower abv, so it freezes more readily – this is why bottled Martinis often freeze solid if stored for an extended period at minus degrees. (For more on Freezer Martinis, **see** *p.92*)

There are pros and cons to using frozen spirits. Dukes Bar in St James's makes its famous Martini with gin poured straight from the freezer – which not only makes the drink wonderfully silky, but also helps to cool the flames of 120ml of pure booze.

For stirred Martinis, though, I find room temperature spirits marry better. I do, however, always use chilled vermouth and a frozen mixing vessel and glass, regardless of the spirit's temperature. (And having said all that, there's usually a bottle of vodka stashed somewhere in my freezer.)

Bartenders will go to great lengths to ensure their Martinis are served cold enough. My friend Hannah Lanfear used to patrol London's Milk & Honey bar zapping guests' drinks with a laser thermometer – if she found one that was too warm, she'd decant the offending cocktail into a freshly-frozen glass.

Bemelmans in New York serves the house Martini in a little decanter nestled in a bowl of crushed ice, so you can be sure it'll be cold to the very last drop, even in the sweltering summertime. Audrey Saunders, formerly of Bemelmans' bar and creator of the Fitty-Fitty (*p.90*), has created a similar set with the excellent bar tool company Cocktail Kingdom (**see** *Retailers p.172*).

Once, at a bar in Barcelona, I had a Martini super-cooled with liquid nitrogen – alas, that ended rather less well, with a pair of pliers and a rather painful olive extraction.

GIN

For a straight-up-and-down Martini, you can't beat a classic London Dry. But gin now comes in a multitude of styles, thanks to the boom in craft distilling.

The one botanical common to them all, by law, is the juniper berry – a little pea-sized fruit (or, strictly, seed cone) with distinctive notes of pepper, citrus, lavender and pine, which grows on a spiky shrub related to the cypress.

Juniper – grows wild in many parts of the world, but most of the berries used to make gin come from Italy and Eastern Europe. They are harvested in the autumn when they've ripened to a deep blue-black, by whacking the bush with a stick. In Tuscany this job is performed by gangs of armed pensioners known as *battitori*. I joined a harvest, once, and that gritty-sweet, resinous taste of sun-baked juniper berries will never leave me.

With the juniper in place, a distiller can choose from a cast of supporting botanicals that's almost infinite. But there are some usual suspects:

Coriander seeds – hard little seeds with tangy citrus and woody notes and a hint of spice.

Orris – derived from the iris root, this has a soft, powdery character, with hints of violet. It's prized by both distillers and perfumers as a 'fixative', as it helps to lock in other botanical notes.

Angelica root – another important fixative, with understated, rather musky/nutty forest-floor aromas.

Lemon and orange peels – these can be used either fresh or dried to achieve a variety of citrus notes, from sherbetty lemon through to bitter marmalade.

Liquorice root – warm, earthy sweetness.

Also: cinnamon-like cassia, peppery cubeb and perfumed cardamom.

There are a number of ways you can make gin, but the most traditional method starts with the botanicals being steeped in neutral grain spirit (which is like a very high-strength, neutral-tasting vodka). This infusion is then heated up in a copper still, which works a bit like a giant kettle. As the temperature rises, the alcohol boils off, taking the botanicals' aromatic flavour compounds with it. These vapours are then captured and condensed back into a spirit.

This spirit, the gin, is then diluted with water to bring it down to bottling strength. In the UK this can range from 37.5% abv to well over 50% abv.

For a Martini, go for something in the 40–47% abv range. Any lower can be a bit under-powered. Any higher is just too punchy.

So-called 'London Dry' gins don't have to be made in London, but they must be made according to certain rules. They have to be juniper-led and all their flavour must come from natural botanicals. All the botanicals must be introduced at distillation stage, and no flavourings or colours can be added thereafter.

This is how the original London-born dry gins such as Beefeater and Tanqueray were (and still are) made – hence the name. The word 'Dry' was there to differentiate them from the sweetened gins popular in the 19th century.

The term is a useful steer on style, and ensures a certain baseline of quality. But there are some great gins that aren't made this way, such as Height of Arrows and Four Pillars Olive Leaf.

CLASSIC LONDON DRY

BEEFEATER LONDON DRY GIN (40% abv) was one of the pioneers of the London Dry style – and it's still going strong in south London after 150 years. Its sherbetty top notes and brisk blast of pine are pitch-perfect in a Martini. A great-value gin that's loved by the trade for its versatility.

TANQUERAY LONDON DRY GIN (41.3% abv) doesn't contain any citrus, so it's much drier and spicier. It has invigorating pepper and cedar notes that make for a wonderfully bracing Martini.

PLYMOUTH GIN (41.2% abv) is London Dry at its most elegant; it has soft notes of rootsy orris, angelica and sweet orange. Distilled at the Black Friars Distillery in Plymouth since 1793, it has the distinction of being the only gin that *The Savoy Cocktail Book* (1930) mentions by name.

NEW-WAVE JUNIPER-FORWARD

I first visited **SIPSMITH** (41.6% abv) in 2009 when it was just starting out in a garage in west London. It's a huge brand now, but remains one of the best of the new-wave London Dry gins, marrying an old-school hit of juniper with lively lemon zest and spice-cupboard notes of cassia and liquorice.

HEPPLE (45% abv) is made on the wild and woolly moors of Northumbria from local juniper, bog myrtle, Douglas Fir, lovage and blackcurrant leaves. It uses a mix of fresh green and dried juniper berries and a combination of old and new distillation techniques to achieve a gin with wonderful harmony and freshness – juniper in HD.

PROCERA BLUE DOT (44% abv) is distilled in Kenya from Juniperus procera, a variety of juniper that only grows in the southern hemisphere. It has a more ethereal character: you taste pine needles, pink pepper and lavender. The beautiful blue glass flask is hand-blown in Kenya.

HEIGHT OF ARROWS (43% abv) is an unusual Scottish gin that's distilled with just one botanical, juniper, and then seasoned with beeswax and salt. The beeswax adds warmth, sweetness and texture; the salt adds a subtle savouriness. A clever creation that's great Martini material but also good just sipped neat.

CITRUSSY

HAYMANS LONDON DRY GIN (41.2% abv) is distilled in London by England's oldest family-owned distillery. It marries classic juniper bite with a star-burst of citrus notes that runs the gamut from juicy and zesty through to thick-cut marmalade.

The sherbetty Japanese yuzu fruit is the star of **KI NO BI** (45.7% abv), a rice-based gin distilled at the Kyoto Distillery. Other Japanese botanicals include sansho pepper, shiso and bamboo leaves. It's a big, bold gin that opens with a dazzling hit of grapefruit and lemongrass, before settling down into more subtle notes of umami-ish green tea.

TANQUERAY NO. TEN (47.3% abv) is distilled with fresh oranges, grapefruits and limes, which give it an extravagant succulence, tempered by more aromatic notes of pepper, basil and chamomile tea. You may want to stir a bit longer just to soften that abv.

If you like tongue-spangling citrus, you should also try **OXLEY COLD DISTILLED LONDON DRY GIN** (47% abv), which has lively, slightly pithy notes of pink grapefruit and orange peel.

SPICY

SACRED GIN (40% abv) is distilled in north London using a high-tech vacuum still that allows its creators Ian and Hilary to capture botanical notes with great delicacy and precision. Its signature botanical is frankincense, which gives it a grand, rather church-y character. It's also big on juniper – complex and sophisticated.

PORTOBELLO ROAD GIN (42% abv) is flavoured with nutmeg and liquorice, which gives it a warm, earthy sweetness. It also has notes of clove-spiked orange, juniper and nose-tickling pepper.

JAISALMER INDIAN CRAFT GIN (43% abv) is distilled in Uttar Pradesh with an array of local ingredients. There's a coriander tang to it like lime pickle, and hints of sweet-and-spicy paan, overlaid with notes of vetiver, lemongrass and orange blossom.

HERBAL/FLORAL

The Scottish isle of Islay is famous for its whisky, but it's also home to **THE BOTANIST** (46% abv), a gin distilled from 22 local plants, including gorse flower, thyme, wood sage, red clover and spearmint. Gloriously fresh and verdant like an armful of wet flowers, it has a finish with finely pixellated notes of bitter lemon peel and herbs.

A walk in a Californian forest inspired the American **ST. GEORGE TERROIR GIN** (45% abv), another craft recipe that leans heavily on local ingredients. It's a real bouquet garni, with notes of oregano, bay, citronella, mint, wormwood, sage, lavender and sweet, rootsy sarsaparilla.

Australia's **FOUR PILLARS OLIVE LEAF GIN** (43.8% abv) is flavoured with olive oil and olive leaf tea, which give it a full-bodied texture and savoury notes of artichoke, sage and green olive. Other antipodean botanicals include macadamia nut, lemon myrtle, rosemary and bay leaf.

Just three botanicals are used to make Wisconsin's **DEATH'S DOOR GIN** (47% abv): organic juniper, coriander and wild fennel. The result is a super-fresh lungful of crunchy fennel bulb, lemon zest, dill, forest pine and pepper.

The Queen of the Night – a cactus flower that blooms in the desert for just one night a year – brings a heady, almost jasmine-like note to **SEVENTY ONE GIN** (40% abv), a golden cask-aged gin that looks, and tastes, like an expensive perfume.

OLD TOM GIN

Before London Dry gin conquered the world, people drank a cordial-style gin called Old Tom, which was sweetened with sugar to make an otherwise rather rough-and-ready spirit more palatable.

A lot of late 19th-century recipes, like the Martinez (*p.96*), would have been made with this – I've tried to adapt and update for London Dry where I can. But if you want to delve deeper into vintage drinks it might be good to have an Old Tom up your sleeve.

HAYMAN'S OLD TOM (41.4% abv) is excellent – cordial-like without being sickly, with notes of sweet orange, lemon balm, aniseed, woody spice and slightly tropical fruitiness.

VODKA

A vodka's raw materials and the way it's distilled can have a big impact on its texture and taste. And the pared-back Martini does a great deal to highlight this.

You can, in theory, distil a vodka from pretty much anything that contains fermentable sugars. Traditional vodka bases include sugar beet, barley, wheat, rye and potatoes. But growing numbers of distillers are now branching out into apples, grapes, milk and even peas.

Vodka's reputation for flavourlessness is down to the fact that a lot of industrial brands are column-distilled to a very high level of purity – which is great from a yield point-of-view (and, helpfully, removes things that might send you blind or kill you) but also strips out a lot of flavour.

Thankfully, more distillers are now putting the emphasis back on taste – using interesting raw ingredients and distillation methods to give their vodkas real character.

RYE

I think rye vodkas are often some of the most interesting: crisp yet substantial, with complex flavours ranging from floral and fruity to nutty and spicy.

Eastern Europe is the heartland of rye vodka. I like **BELVEDERE** (40% abv) from Poland. It's very polished, with pretty notes of cream soda, sugared almond and white flowers up top, and more peppery, earthiness beneath. The finish is smooth, with a very slight saltiness. (Belvedere also does a duo of Single Estate vodkas made with rye grown in different places – if you think vodka can't express terroir, you might find these interesting.)

WHEAT

Wheat vodkas tend to be crisp, clean and often slightly sweet.

GREY GOOSE (40% abv) is made with winter wheat grown in the same part of France favoured by many of the country's top bakers. It gives the vodka luxurious notes of crème pâtissière and freshly baked baguette. The finish is nice and silky with just a hint of cracked black pepper.

MIXED GRAIN

KONIK'S TAIL (40% abv) is made in Poland from a blend of spelt, wheat and rye – cereals that are grown near the ancient Białowieża Forest where the wild Konik ponies graze. The grain character really comes through in this one – at its core it's nutty, almost dark chocolate-y. But the start and finish are elegant, fresh and creamy.

DIMA'S (40% abv) is an old-style Ukrainian vodka distilled just outside the capital, Kyiv. I got to know its creator, Dima Deinega, in the weeks following Russia's invasion of Ukraine in 2022 and have been a fan ever since. Locally grown barley, wheat and rye give it a big, bold personality and just a hint of umami – a great partner for the pickles vodka is often served with in Eastern Europe.

EIGHT LANDS ORGANIC SPEYSIDE VODKA (42% abv) is a family-owned vodka made in the heart of Scotch whisky country. It's distilled in a copper pot still (rather than the usual column still) from organic barley and wheat, and bottled at a higher-than-average 42% abv, which gives it great structure and spicy intensity.

POTATO VODKA

Potato vodkas are about texture as much as they are about taste. They're characteristically full-bodied with a starchy creaminess like buttered mashed potato.

The 100-year-old Polish brand **LUKSUSOWA** (40% abv) combines that fluffy mash character with a fresh, almost chalky minerality. **CHOPIN** (40% abv), also from Poland, has a luxurious creaminess like white chocolate.

PORTOBELLO ROAD BRITISH POTATO VODKA (40% abv) has much bigger bones – it's almost oily in texture, with rootsy, savoury notes like baked potato skin. Great in a Dirty Martini.

RICE

The Japanese rice vodka **HAKU** (40% abv) is delicate and pristine, with subtle notes of white marshmallow and spring flowers. Handle with care as its tiny voice can easily be drowned out by other ingredients.

OTHER THINGS

Growing numbers of more eco-conscious distillers are now making vodka from peas, a crop that helps to 'fix' nitrogen in the soil and restore its fertility. **POD PEA VODKA** (40% abv) from Manchester has a limey, grassy, mineral flavour, almost like a blanco tequila. (Its green glass bottle, made from British sand, has also been designed to reduce its carbon footprint.) **NÀDAR** (43% abv) is made at Arbikie, a Scottish field-to-bottle distillery that's a real pioneer in sustainability. It's slightly rounder, with a more floral sweetness.

BLACK COW VODKA (40% abv) is made in Dorset from the whey left over after cheese-making, which gives it the luxurious fatness of clotted cream. The merest hint of farmyard funk adds personality. Gorgeous sipping.

VERMOUTH

Vermouth is constantly being muscled out of the Martini. It's high time we brought it back in, because it's a magnificent drink in its own right, and not just a cipher to gin.

It's part of a family of aperitifs technically known as 'aromatised wines', which are wines that have been flavoured with botanicals, sweetened with sugar and lightly fortified.

Its signature botanical is wormwood, a frilly, silver-green herb that combines a face-puckering bitterness with aromatic notes of minted peas and sage. It's from the German word for wormwood, *wermut*, that vermouth gets its name. In the EU, all vermouths must be flavoured with wormwood by law.

Wormwood has been used as a herbal remedy, preservative and piquant flavouring for wine since at least 1000 BC. Its hallmark bitterness made it prized above all as a digestive.

Vermouth, proper, was born in the 18th century in the Italian city of Turin. It was originally designed as a health tonic, but locals grew to love its bittersweet taste. And it quickly became the toast of the city's fashionable cafés.

By the middle of the 19th century brands such as Cinzano, Martini and Noilly Prat had begun arriving on American shores, and this paved the way for a whole new genre of mixed drinks made with spirits and vermouth, the most famous examples being the Martini, the Manhattan and the Martinez.

Most vermouths, whatever their colour, are made from a white wine base (one exception is Chazalettes Rosso, which is made from the red barbera grape). Any colour usually comes from the addition of a little flavourless caramel colouring or a tint from the botanicals.

The thing that really determines the character of a vermouth is the mix of botanicals the blender uses. And most vermouths contain well over a dozen different herbs, peels, flowers and spices. Ingredients can range from orange zest, lemon balm, mint, cinnamon, cloves, lavender, rose, saffron, sandalwood, rhubarb and raspberry, to vine flowers, nutmeg, dandelion, allspice, angelica, aloe, vanilla and cloves. I've had vermouth flavoured with myrrh, hops, honey and even oyster shells.

Vermouth can be white, gold, amber, ruby-red, or pink as Provençal rosé, and taste herbal and dry, nutty and golden, or as rich and spicy as Christmas cake.

It's a ready-made cocktail in a bottle; a drinkable perfume. So, please, next time you mix a Martini, try to give the vermouth a little more room.

A NOTE ON STORAGE

Vermouth is wine-based and therefore deteriorates like wine when exposed to light and oxygen (albeit at a slower rate). It doesn't 'go off' exactly, it just gets duller, like a slice of apple going brown, and loses its bright top notes.

To slow its rate of decline, store it out of direct light and keep open bottles in the fridge. Vermouth stored like this should remain in peak condition for eight to 12 weeks. (It will remain perfectly drinkable – if not quite Martini-worthy – for several months after that. Once it's totally knackered it can still be really useful in the kitchen.) The paler, drier styles tend to be the most delicate.

If you take ages to finish a bottle, consider decanting it into several smaller ones, as this reduces the amount of surface area in sustained contact with damaging oxygen. When buying vermouth always go for the smallest format possible – Cocchi, for example, sells its dry vermouth by the very dainty 50cl bottle.

DRY VERMOUTH

Light gold or colourless, this is the driest style of all – the default for a Dry Martini. Sometimes referred to as 'French vermouth' as it was popularised by France.

My fridge is never without a bottle of **NOILLY PRAT DRY** (18% abv) – the *non plus ultra* of Martini vermouths. Oak-aged white wines give it a golden colour and nutty flavour a bit like sherry. Mediterranean herbs, sweet lemon peel and a hint of saltiness add mouthwatering complexity.

MARTINI EXTRA DRY (15% abv) is fresh and pure – grassy, citrussy, even a bit pleasantly soapy, with a fine line of bitterness that runs right the way through. Good if you want a Martini that's really pristine, or when mixing with very delicate spirits.

COCCHI EXTRA DRY (17% abv) is really dry, but also wonderfully aromatic – lemon and lime, parched thyme, lemon balm, citrus peels, spicy woods and a big crunch of savoury celery.

SACRED ENGLISH DRY VERMOUTH (21.8% abv) was created specially for the ultra-dry Martinis at Dukes (*p.86*) – so a little goes a long way. Big on wormwood character and pungent herbal flavours.

DOLIN DRY (17.5% abv) is made with Savoie white wines and herbs picked in the Alps, which give it a meadow-y character and a gentle bitterness.

VAULT COASTAL DRY VERMOUTH (17.6% abv), AKA 'Champagne and Oysters', is flavoured with oyster shells, olive leaves, Amalfi lemons and rock samphire foraged in England. Fresh, mineral, lean – vermouth at its most exhilarating.

WHITE VERMOUTH

Colourless or golden, this is the sweetest vermouth style. Characterised by notes of vanilla and citrus. Also known as bianco, blanc or blanco, depending on what country you're in.

DOLIN BLANC (16% abv) is fragrant and floral with talc-y notes of rose and violet. There are some fleshier white nectarine characters balanced by minimal bitterness.

CINZANO BIANCO (15% abv) is crystal-clear with an intense cream-soda sweetness. There's an edge of tart, bitter lemon sorbet, however, that just about saves it. Famously advertised by Joan Collins and Leonard Rossiter in the 1970s.

The golden **MARTINI BIANCO** (15% abv) marries thick, honeyed sweetness with a pleasantly medicinal hit. The creamy caress of nougat cut with the bite of a malaria pill.

CHAZALETTES BIANCO (16.5% abv) is wonderfully characterful – you really get that sage-y wormwood scent. Its tongue-coating sweetness is counterbalanced by woody, spicy notes. There are bitter herbs and bronze autumn apples, plus a wisp of vanilla tobacco smoke.

AMBER VERMOUTH

A lesser-spotted style, with the complexity of a dry but the fuller body of a white. If a Martini is tasting a little too austere, a drop of amber will often put it right.

From Italy comes **MANCINO BIANCO** (16% abv), a pale gold, viscous ambrato, with notes of dried apricot and clove-studded orange and a dry, woody finish pleasantly reminiscent of spicy aftershave.

MARTINI RISERVA SPECIALE AMBRATO (18% abv), from Martini's upmarket Riserva range, is also excellent – very silky, aromatic and dense, with notes of toasted nuts, sweet cinnamon rolls, bitter herbs and golden marmalade.

ROSÉ VERMOUTH

This modern, fruity/floral style of vermouth doesn't make an appearance in this book, but two I like are Belsazar Rosé from Germany and the sherry-based Rosé by Spanish sherry producer Lustau. The aperitifs Lillet Rosé and Cocchi Rosa – while not technically vermouths as they're not bittered with wormwood – are also good.

RED VERMOUTH

Red or tawny in colour, this style of vermouth is used in many of the proto-Martinis. Often referred to as 'Italian vermouth' or, rather unhelpfully, 'sweet vermouth', despite the fact that it's not the sweetest (white vermouth is).

MARTINI ROSSO (15% abv) is seen as too mainstream by some, but a lot of bartenders like it because it's not too overbearing. Tawny red, with a light caramel nuttiness and notes of dried fruits and bitter orange.

MARTINI RISERVA SPECIALE RUBINO (18% abv) is more complex with a plummy mulled-wine fruitiness and notes of bitter chocolate and sage.

MANCINO ROSSO AMARANTO (16% abv) takes it to the dark side with intense notes of cacao, coffee and bittermint, balanced by zesty orange and a rich sweetness.

SACRED ENGLISH SPICED VERMOUTH (18% abv) is flavoured with 26 botanicals including earthy-sweet rhubarb, orange zest, cloves, thyme and wormwood. The recipe was inspired by clove-spiked oranges, or pomanders, and has an almost amaro-like bitterness.

The barbera-based **CHAZALETTES ROSSO DELLA REGINA VERMOUTH** (16.5% abv) is one of the few vermouths to be based on red, rather than white, wine. It layers red and black fruits with spicy woods, resinous incense and parched herbs – generous and beautifully balanced.

OTHER APERITIFS

Filed alongside vermouth you'll find another family of wine-based aperitifs bittered with gentian and quinine. While these are not technically vermouths – as they don't contain wormwood – they can also be used to aromatise a Martini. Two in particular are worth mentioning:

The original Vesper Martini (*p.83*) was made with a French aperitif called Kina Lillet, which is now extinct. Its less bitter descendant **LILLET BLANC** (17% abv) is made with Bordeaux white wines, fruit liqueurs and quinine. It can be tweaked to taste something like the original Kina Lillet by adding a drop of Angostura Bitters.

The Italian answer to Lillet is **COCCHI AMERICANO BIANCO** (16.5% abv), an aperitivo that's made from a blend of Piedmont white wines, cinchona, gentian and citrus. Honeyed, refreshing and thrillingly bitter all at once, it is also excellent in a Vesper Martini or the Alberto Cocktail (*p.113*).

BITTERS

Quite a few recipes in this book call for orange bitters. Three brands I like are Angostura, The Bitter Truth and Regan's.

ANGOSTURA ORANGE BITTERS are woody, spicy and sweet, like thick-cut marmalade.

THE BITTER TRUTH ORANGE BITTERS from Germany have a more high-toned zestiness, like freshly torn orange peel.

REGAN'S ORANGE BITTERS, created by the late, great bartender Gary Regan, have an aromatic bittersweetness closer to Campari.

For recipes that call for straight-up aromatic bitters, I use classic Angostura Bitters.

A NOTE ON BRANDS

I tested all the gin-based Martinis in this book with Beefeater, because it's versatile, widely available and good value. My benchmark vodka was Belvedere. If a recipe called for a specific brand, however, I tested it with that, too, wherever possible. For vermouths, I had to chop and change a bit, because they're all so different, but two brands I used a lot were Noilly Prat and Martini. In the instances when only one brand will do, such as Luxardo Maraschino Liqueur, I have named it.

Some companies provided me with stock for recipe-testing, but I wasn't paid in money or kind to include any products in this book. Any brands mentioned are simply there because I think they are good.

GARNISH

If you've ever agonised over whether to have an olive or twist in your Martini, you will know the importance of this step. Because once you commit to the garnish, there is no going back.

TWIST

A Martini with a lemon twist is dazzling and clean – a starburst of citrussy zest. There is a sense of renewal with every sip; a tiny moment of revelation.

Dukes scents its Martinis with lemons from Amalfi (often presented, in a rather painterly way, with the leaves still attached). I've also used bergamot, the bitter green orange used to scent Earl Grey tea. November to January is the season for yuzu, that wonderfully knobbly yellow citrus fruit from Japan, which fuses lemongrass, grapefruit, lemon and mandarin in one heavenly perfume.

Simply swapping lemon for orange can be enough to give your Martini a whole new accent. Try the Marguerite (*p.98*), or the Flame of Love (*p.117*) if you like pyrotechnics. Grapefruit, which is more pithy and pungent, imparts a citric jolt of electricity. A very fine twist of lime, with its intense bitter greenness and scent of damp flowers, can also be good if used sparingly.

Always choose fruits that are nice and fresh – the skin should be taut with citrus oils. And go for unwaxed fruit, if you have the choice.

HOW TO DO A TWIST...

Take a sharp paring knife or speed-peeler, and cut a thumb-sized strip of zest (if you want an immaculate twist you can always tidy up the edges afterwards). Or simply plane off a coin-sized piece of peel from the fruit's edge.

Hold the piece of peel shiny side-down over your Martini and give it a sharp pinch, so the scented oils are expressed across the surface of the drink. I like to anoint the rim of the glass with the twist as well – although some find this a bit bitter.

The bartenders at the Connaught pour their Martinis from a great height and scent the column of liquid as it's falling – a feat which, I can attest, is as tricky as patting your head and rubbing your tummy at the same time.

You then have a choice: either drop the twist into the drink or discard it (as Milk & Honey's Sasha Petraske used to say: 'turn it and burn it'). This is another apparently innocuous detail that can get Martini lovers very heated.

A Martini with a discarded twist tends to be more delicately scented. A Martini with the twist left in to infuse acquires more notes of bitter lemon. I rather like that bit of pithy punctuation, as well as the pop of colour. But if I'm having an olive as well (which, believe it or not, is allowed) I tend to discard, or the glass just gets too crowded.

If you don't have fresh fruit, or want to cut down on waste, the Cocktail Elements citrus essences by Linden Leaf are a good substitute. Available in lemon, orange, lime and yuzu, they can be spritzed on your Martini just like a scent.

ACCOUTREMENTS

The twist delivers its charms upfront. The olive is more about promise. The mere sight of it, saltily steeping away, is enough to get your mouth watering.

The cliché is a mushy, grey-green specimen stuffed with a red pimento pepper. But the king of Martini olives, in my mind, is the Sicilian nocellara. This glossy, bright green marble has toothsome flesh that's grassy, fruity and buttery. I like two or three in my Martini, and I like them with the stone left in so I can do a bit of gnawing. A few extra in a little dish on the side is also always welcome.

Black olives, while less traditional, also have their place in a Martini, especially in twists containing sweet liqueurs or absinthe (**see** *Obituary – p.110*).

Sometimes, the olive oversteps its boundaries – and the result is a Dirty Martini. **See** *p.84* for some thoughts on how to stop this situation getting messy.

PICKLES

Brined olives add saltiness to a Martini. Vinegar-steeped pickles add more of a tang. The pickled onion, famously, is the hallmark of the Gibson (*p.78*).

Hemingway liked his Martini onions frozen to -15°C. (He also liked fresh onion, finely sliced, which sounds like some kind of repulsive initiation drink to me.) The food writer MFK Fisher served her guests Martinis garnished with olives stuffed with tiny silverskins – exquisite but fiddly.

The Martini suits pickles of all kinds: beetroot, cornichons, caperberries. Pickled walnuts and hazelnuts were briefly fashionable around the turn of the 20th century.

If you're an adept home-pickler, you might like to try bartender Nick Strangeway's suggestion of a Gibson with a tiny, pickled gooseberry. I also love the BAO-tini (*p.146*), which is garnished with an electric-pink radish pickled in Chinese vinegar and chilli.

OTHER ACCOUTREMENTS

The olive and twist will always reign supreme, but you'll find lots more unusual garnishes in this book: cucumber ribbons, apple slices, olive oil, salt.

The earliest Martinis, which were generally sweet, were often garnished with cherries. I have to say, though, I find all this stickiness decidedly un-Martini. If you're not sure what garnish to go for, try picking out a keynote in the gin and asking yourself: if I was cooking with this ingredient what would I pair it with? If it was a fennel-led gin like Death's Door, for example, you could look to Sicilian salads, which often pair fennel with orange slices and salty black olives. (Niki Segnit's *The Flavour Thesaurus* is a brilliant source of flavour-matching ideas.)

There have been a few attempts to give the Martini a 'rim' a bit like a Margarita. Atom bomb creator J. Robert Oppenheimer liked his Martini ultra-dry in a glass edged with lime juice and honey. The Argentinian answer to the Martini, the Clarito, is served in a coupe wiped with lemon and dipped in sugar.

SNACKS

The Martini is a drink that abhors clutter – but it loves a retinue of snacks. It's one of the very few cocktails that's an excellent food match.

The perfect foil for its searing purity is lots of salt and fat – crisps and charcuterie or, even better, something really decadent. At the chintzy Bemelmans Bar in Manhattan you can order your Martini with a side of truffle fries so hot they burn your fingers; at the Connaught guests slum it over five-star Martinis and oozing slices of pizza.

An airport Martini with a burger is a very singular pleasure – a collision of red blood and cold booze that leaves you stunned and fortified in equal measure.

Steak tartare, ceviche, sashimi – the Martini loves food that's on the edge. A really dry Martini and a couple of oysters can be as reviving as a winter skinny-dip (if you like oysters, **see** the *Spring Forward Martini* on *p.157*).

Olives and pickles are excellent – but that probably goes without saying. Dante in New York gives you a whole array of 'accoutrements', as it calls them, to play with.

High Five in Tokyo serves a different snack with every drink: a thimble of sweet potato shards, a wafer of Iberico ham carved at the bar, a mouthful of Brie atop a tiny biscuit. Every morsel that arrives is like a beat that keeps time across an evening of drinking.

Off the Record is an old-school hotel bar not far from the White House in Washington DC. When I had an (absolutely vast) Martini there it came with a very presidential silver dish of jelly beans.

The Martini is so versatile it'll even partner with other drinks: it's great with a champagne chaser or book-ended by two beers in a so-called 'Martini sandwich'.

The perfect accompaniment should whet the appetite, rather than sate it entirely. Because a Martini always tastes best when you are a little bit hungry.

EQUIPMENT

THE GLASS

You can't tell a whole lot about a Martini simply by looking at it – so the glass does a very important job of setting the tone. It can make the drink seem old-fashioned, futuristic, whimsical or utilitarian.

The Y-shaped glass most of us think of when we say 'Martini' made its debut in 1925 in Paris at the Exposition Internationale des Arts Décoratifs et Industriels Modernes – a design showcase regarded by many as art deco's birthplace.

The vessel's crisp, clean lines and angular shape were a big departure from the cocktail glasses of the day, which had hitherto been shaped much more like a wine glass, and were much more ornate.

The glass's creator, Austrian architect Oswald Haerdtl, actually intended it to be used for champagne. But as its popularity spread it was quickly hijacked by the cocktail of the age.

Its distinctive Y-shaped silhouette became international short-hand for cocktails – for sophistication and fun. It was patterned out round the world in print and on film and in countless neon bar signs. Today, there are just two emojis for 'cocktail', and the Martini glass is one.

The glass's image went a bit downmarket in the 1980s, when the name 'Martini' was conferred on any Y-shaped cocktail, regardless of how tacky it was. More recently, though, it's had a renaissance thanks to glass companies like Richard Brendon and Kimura who have re-imagined Haerdtl's original design in hair-raisingly fine crystal.

I'm also a big fan of the curvaceous coupe – it's so timelessly elegant. It's often claimed those graceful lines were modelled on the breasts of Marie Antoinette – it's a myth, alas, but once someone tells you this, it's hard to forget.

A super coupe for everyday is Urban Bar's 150ml Retro Champagne Glass Coupette – it has perfect proportions, is robust enough to withstand a party and retails for just £8.50.

Another great all-rounder glass is the Nick & Nora, a mid-century design that was named after Nick and Nora Charles, the Martini-swigging sleuths in the post-Prohibition flick *The Thin Man*. It's a bit more upright than a coupe and slightly more capacious – nice if you like your Martini, as I do, with more than one olive. It's a generic style, these days – a lot of glass companies do one.

SIZE MATTERS

A mistake people often make when serving Martinis is using a glass that's way too big, so the cocktail's all warm, and the drinker totally smashed, before they're even halfway finished. It's much better to keep your Martinis icy and small. That first, electrifying sip is usually the best one, after all.

The earliest cocktails were tiny – typically a very dainty 75–90ml. I've seen pictures of Hemingway sipping Martinis not much bigger than a thimble. By the middle of the 20th century, cocktail glasses had doubled in size; and by the 1980s they were topping out at a truly grotesque half pint.

The perfect-sized Martini glass, in my mind, is somewhere between 100ml and 170ml. This is smaller than average, but I've recommended some good retailers on *p.172*. Those little liqueur glasses you often see in charity shops and flea markets can also be good.

Always, always, always freeze your glass before using it. Polish with a microfibre cloth. And hold by the stem so your fingers don't warm your Martini up.

TOOLS

You can busk a decent Martini without any specialist tools at all. But a few good bits of kit will really help take it to the next level.

JIGGER

The traditional nip-waisted jigger is a bit of a blunt instrument for Martinis – you want a tool capable of much more accurate measuring.

The Easy Jigger by Difford's is brilliant – it has a funnel-shaped design that does imperial and metric measures from 1.25ml right up to 60ml, and many increments in between. The numbers run up the inside, which makes it much easier to pour to the requisite line. It also has a foot on the bottom, so you can leave it hanging upside down on the rim of the mixing glass while sticky liqueurs and syrups ooze out in their own sweet time.

MIXING GLASS

The tin or glass half of a Boston shaker (**see** *p.56*) works just fine as a mixing vessel. But a really beautiful mixing glass will make the preparation of a Martini feel much more ceremonial.

The Rolls-Royce of mixing glasses are the mouth-blown ones by Japanese company Yarai, which have a 'seamless' design that's meant to make your stirring almost silent. The one I have is just about small enough to pour one-handed, but big enough to stir two Martinis at a time. It has a diamond pattern cut into the base that glints beautifully in candlelight. A Yarai glass will set you back £40–£50. In the UK, Urban Bar (**see** *p.172*) does a more affordable version that's also great.

LONG-HANDLED BAR SPOON

A long-handled bar spoon makes stirring easier and a lot more elegant – for more on technique, **see** *Method – p.58*.

Bar spoons can also be used for measuring 5ml of liquid, or a 'bar spoon' in cocktail parlance. They're also handy for scooping olives. In addition, some bar spoons have a flat end that can be used for muddling herbs and fruit.

SHAKER

The shaker I use is a Boston, which is a two-piece design, comprising a glass and a tin (or, sometimes, two tins) that fit together to create one long Zeppelin. Bostons are great because they can be used for shaken and stirred drinks, and are robust, cheap and easy to clean. For all these reasons, the Boston tends to be the shaker used most widely by the trade.

I use the glass half for stirring drinks, because I like to see what I am doing. But Dave Arnold's *Liquid Intelligence* makes a strong case for using the tin, because it has a much lower specific heat capacity than glass so requires less energy to cool or heat. Unless you're banging out dozens of Martinis a night, though, this shouldn't be a problem.

HAWTHORN STRAINER

If you use a Boston shaker or a mixing glass, you will also need a Hawthorn strainer, which is a tennis racquet-shaped stainless steel tool that fits over the mouth of the vessel and holds back the ice as you pour.

DROPPER BOTTLES WITH PIPETTES

A lot of recipes in this book call for drops and dashes of things such as tinctures and absinthe – you'll find dispensing these much easier if you decant them into a little dropper bottle with a pipette.

COCKTAIL PICKS

I filed these under 'nice to have' in my last book, *The Cocktail Edit*, but in the case of the Martini I'd consider them *essential*. Because no one wants to see you fishing the olive out of your pristine drink with a grubby finger.

Wooden cocktail picks set my teeth on edge; I like picks cast in clinical stainless steel. They make Martinis look smart and imbue them with a pleasing whiff of danger.

And picks can be very hazardous, as the novelist Sherwood Anderson discovered to his cost. He inadvertently swallowed a cocktail pick while drinking a Martini in 1941 and died from acute peritonitis.

SOME USEFUL MEASUREMENTS

25ml = single shot

50ml = double shot

5ml = 1 teaspoon/bar spoon

1.25ml = 15 drops approx

METHOD

THE PERFECT MARTINI

The perfect Martini formula is wrangled over endlessly – but that is all part of the fun. Is it better mixed 6:2, 50/50 or, à la Hemingway, a rasping 15:1?

The ratio is just the start of your problems. The choice of spirits, the mode of preparation and the garnish are all important considerations, too. A study of the Martini conducted by mixologists Claire Warner and Tristan Stephenson identified no fewer than 21 different variables.

Do the maths, and this means you could potentially mix 6.9 quadrillion different Martinis. Yet not one, in this whole Milky Way of drinks, will be considered perfect by everybody.

And that definition of 'perfect' will change depending on a variety of things including the season, the setting, the company and, sometimes, how bad your day has been.

I don't believe in One True Recipe. But I do believe there's a preferable method; a way of doing things that will ensure your Martini tastes a bit better:

FROZEN GLASS – A frozen glass will instantly upgrade virtually any mixed drink – so if you only take away one thing away from this book, make it this.

ICE – Ice is a tool *and* an ingredient – so always use lots of fresh, clean, odour-free ice for shaking and stirring.

GOOD INGREDIENTS – Expensive ingredients aren't necessary, but sound quality is. If in doubt, stick to classic brands such as Beefeater, Tanqueray, Plymouth, Noilly Prat and Martini. Keep your vermouth in good condition by storing it properly (**see** *p.34*).

GARNISH – The garnish has the power to make a Martini or absolutely sink it. So give it some thought – use nice, fresh citrus and respectable olives.

TIME – A Martini's window of perfection is fleeting, so it helps to have a routine (**see** *p.70*). And once it's mixed, drink immediately.

SHAKEN, STIRRED
... OR THROWN?

There are a number of ways you can mix a Martini, each with its own benefits. The important thing is to do what you like – but just know *why* you do it.

When you stir, shake or throw a Martini with ice you're not just mixing the ingredients – you're also lowering their temperature, raising the level of dilution and introducing some aeration.

Coldness makes a Martini more silky and dense, but it also suppresses aroma and flavour. It can mask some of the alcoholic 'burn', creating the impression of a drink that's smoother.

Dilution and aeration make a Martini fresher and lighter; it helps the botanicals to breathe, so you end up with a drink that's a bit more nuanced, but with less intensity.

Locating the sweet spot between all these things is a case of trial and error. But if you want to go deep into the physics of it all, Dave Arnold's *Liquid Intelligence* gets very granular.

And it's not solely a question of science; it's also a question of theatre. The way a Martini's prepared can radically alter the energy of both drink and drinker. The busy rattle of a shaker, the meditative whirring of a spoon – these are all important ingredients in the experience too.

STIRRED

A stirred Martini, in my mind, is the best of all worlds. You've loosened its stays just enough that it can breathe, but it's still got intensity and poise.

Give your mixing vessel a blast in the freezer for a couple of minutes first, so it's really, really cold (I'm so devoted to this step I keep my mixing glass in the freezer, permanently). If you haven't done so already, this is also the moment to freeze your cocktail glass.

If you don't have room in your freezer, fill your mixing vessel two-thirds with ice and stir for 30 seconds or so to chill it. Tip off any melt water, top up with fresh ice and add your ingredients.

Nestle the bar spoon down among the ice cubes until it touches the bottom, and then give it a gentle nudge to get the contents moving. Aim for a seamless spinning action, rather than clunky mixing. The ideal stirring time will depend on the strength of the gin, the volume of ice and your own personal taste, but a good rule of thumb is between 20 and 30 seconds.

The perfect stir takes practice. But the way you hold your bar spoon can help (**see** *p.64*).

TWO WAYS TO STIR

1. THE PRO WAY: As taught to me by Ago Perrone at The Connaught Bar. Make a gun shape with your hand and then lay the spoon diagonally across your extended index and middle finger, so the shaft passes under your thumb at the top, and over the top of your closed ring finger at the bottom. Close your fingers lightly around the spoon and insert it diagonally into the ice, so the tip is resting in the corner of the glass and the top of the spoon is in line with the centre of the vessel, so it acts like a spindle. If you hold the spoon very lightly, and keep the top of the spoon central at all times, you shouldn't need to keep adjusting it as you stir.

2. THE CHEAT'S WAY: Turn the bar spoon upside down and use the straight end (this also works with a chopstick, the handle of a fork or a pen).

SHAKEN

This is the Martini in a more upbeat mood – lighter, softer and more refreshing. All the little shards of ice and bubbles floating around in it may also make it seem a bit 'busier'.

A Martini that's shaken for too long, though, can be horribly insipid. So shake hard and fast, with masses of ice, for no more than five or six seconds.

The shaken Martini has had its ups and downs over the course of history. The Bradford (*p.78*) – which is basically a Dry Martini with bitters, shaken – can be traced back to the turn of the 20th century. *The Savoy Cocktail Book* (1930) also features quite a few Martini variations that are shaken.

James Bond first uttered the immortal words 'shaken not stirred' in Ian Fleming's novel *Diamond Are Forever*, published in 1956. But the secret agent's signature shaken Martini, the Vesper (*p.83*), debuted in *Casino Royale*, which was published three years earlier.

Fleming was a cocktail aficionado, and it's been theorised that he made Bond a fan of shaken Martinis precisely because it went against the grain; it cast Bond as a daring bon viveur with a flagrant disregard for conventions of the day.

THROWN

This showboaty technique sees the Martini poured back and forth in a great arc between two tins. Advocates maintain it produces a drink with finer, more sustained aeration.

Mixographer Jared Brown believes it may have been the way the original Martini was made, because 'the earliest-known mention of a cocktail shaker, in 1869, described it being used to throw as well as shake.' It's an art still practised at Barcelona's historic Boadas cocktail bar.

It's not a technique I have mastered, so here are Jared Brown's instructions:

'Combine your ingredients in an empty tin or mixing glass. Fill another tin or mixing glass right to the top with ice. Pour in the drink. Place a julep strainer over the ice and hold it in place with one finger. Raise both the empty and full tins or mixing glasses above your head. (If you are using mixing glasses, be sure the pour spout is backwards as it will interfere with the flow of the liquid when you throw.)

Begin to pour from the full one to the empty one, lowering the empty one as far as you can reach, and never taking your eyes off the one that is catching the liquid. (The moment you try to look at the one that's holding the ice, you'll end up with the drink on your shoes.)

Before the pour has finished, bring the catch vessel back up so that the stream finishes with the two close together again. Pour the drink through the julep strainer and back into the ice. Repeat. Depending on the quality of the ice, the handle of the julep strainer will rise after a few or many throws. Think of this as the pop-up timer that lets you know when the drink is done.'

DIRECT

This method sees frozen spirits poured 'direct' from bottle to glass without shaking or stirring with ice first. The result is a Martini that's gloriously silky and dense but also incredibly strong.

The direct method was popularised by Dukes Bar in St James's (**see** *p.86*) – a spot frequented by many celebrated Martini lovers, including Bond author Ian Fleming.

TASTING AND ADJUSTING

If you're not sure whether your Martini's *à point*, by all means taste and adjust before you pour it – this is considered perfectly acceptable practice and you'll often see bartenders do it. The most polite way to do this is to scoop a bit out with a bar spoon and taste it off the back of your hand. If you put the spoon to your lips, replace it with a fresh one before you put it back in.

RUNNING ORDER

1. PUT YOUR COCKTAIL GLASS AND MIXING VESSEL IN THE FREEZER (OR FILL BOTH WITH ICE AND LEAVE TO STAND FOR A FEW MINUTES, TO CHILL).

2. CLEAR THE DECK OF CLUTTER, AND THE IMMEDIATE VICINITY OF PLAINTIVE CHILDREN, PETS THAT NEED TO GO OUT, ETC. TURN OFF ANY DISTRACTING ELECTRONIC GADGETS. MAYBE EVEN PUT ON A RECORD OR LIGHT A FEW CANDLES.

3. ASSEMBLE YOUR BAR TOOLS AND INGREDIENTS, AND ANYTHING YOU NEED FOR THE GARNISH.

4. REMOVE THE MIXING VESSEL FROM THE FREEZER, FILL IT TWO-THIRDS WITH ICE AND ADD YOUR INGREDIENTS.

5. STIR OR SHAKE AS REQUIRED.

6. TASTE AND ADJUST IF NECESSARY.

7. EXTRACT YOUR COCKTAIL GLASS FROM THE FREEZER AND STRAIN THE MARTINI INTO IT.

8. GARNISH.

9. SIT DOWN, HAVE A SIP AND SAVOUR THE MOMENT.

MARTINIS FOR PARTIES

If I'm doing Martinis for lots of people, then I'll knock up a batch of pre-mixed Freezer Martinis (*p.92*), which can be poured direct from bottle to glass without any faffing with ice and bar tools. They can be prepped days, or even weeks, in advance and then stored in the freezer. A single 70cl bottle will serve about seven people.

(I once went to a really big party in the wilds of Northumbria where pre-mixed Hepple Martinis were dispensed from big glass demi-johns. It was a freezing cold night, and we were in a marquee, so keeping them cold wasn't a problem.)

You're unlikely to have enough freezer space to freeze an entire party's-worth of cocktail glasses. So, just set them out on a tray and fill them with ice and a splash of water and leave them to stand for five to ten minutes (and then obviously, before you use a glass, chuck the melted ice away).

Olives are the easiest *en masse* garnish. If you're going twist, use coin-sized pieces of lemon peel. I've witnessed bartenders cutting these little yellow discs on an industrial scale. In an ideal world, these would be cut at the last possible moment, but we're after efficiency here – so prepare your twists an hour or two in advance and store in plastic containers in the fridge.

A good alternative to fresh lemons would be one of Cocktail Elements' citrus sprays by Linden Leaf. You could even set out a choice of flavours and let your guests spritz their Martinis themselves.

For fear of stating the bleeding obvious: Martinis are very strong. So keep 'em small and lay on lots of food to keep your guests propped up.

RECIPES

CLASSIC

Every recipe in this chapter stays true to the holy trinity of gin (or vodka), dry vermouth and bitters. They are all Martinis in the truest sense – just with small, but important, tweaks.

DRY MARTINI

GLASS: *cocktail glass*

GARNISH: *twist and/or olive*

METHOD: *stir with ice and strain*

50ml gin

10ml dry vermouth

1 dash orange bitters (optional)

The perfect Dry Martini is a matter of taste, but it's also a state of mind – a sort of platonic ideal that Martini lovers can end up questing for their entire lives.

We've got to start somewhere, though, so let's start with 5:1 – a ratio of gin to vermouth that you'll often get if you order a Dry Martini in a bar. I like 5:1 because it's precise and fresh, but you can still definitely taste the vermouth. The more austere 7:1 is a bit harder on the maths, but also good.

My ur-Martini is made with a London Dry gin; I want that juniper hit to the fore. For the vermouth, I vacillate between Noilly Prat Dry and the fresher-style extra drys by Cocchi and Martini.

Old-style Martinis featured a dash of orange bitters; I rather like this touch. I'm also firmly of the view that a Dry Martini should always be stirred.

The garnish is a vexed question – for more on the subject, see *p.43*. For what it's worth, I quite like a lemon twist, discarded, *and* an olive – which I know some people find a bit shocking.

GIBSON

GLASS: *cocktail glass or rocks*

GARNISH: *pickled silverskin onions*

METHOD: *stir with ice and strain or serve on the rocks*

50ml gin or vodka
10ml dry vermouth
5ml pickled onion brine (optional)

Who gave the Gibson its pickled onion? No one knows for sure. But this Martini twist was reputedly named after the American illustrator Charles Dana Gibson. 'The onions represent the milky white breasts of the women he drew,' writes bartender Dick Bradsell, 'so always give the client two.'

It's thought the onion was added to distinguish the Gibson from regular Martinis, which were made with a dash of orange bitters up until Prohibition. So the onions are in, and the bitters out. But you've still got room for manoeuvre. A Gibson's rather good on the rocks. And it's also nice made with vodka.

BRADFORD

GLASS: *cocktail glass*

GARNISH: *lemon twist, discarded*

METHOD: *shake with ice and strain*

50ml gin
5ml dry vermouth
1 dash orange bitters

A Bradford is basically just a bitters-laced Martini that's been shaken rather than stirred. The result is deceptively zingy and light; the Martini at its most dangerous.

History doesn't relate who Bradford was, or why he liked his Martinis shaken. But a similar drink appears in Harry Johnson's *Bartenders' Manual* (1900), under the name Bradford à la Martini: it calls for equal parts Old Tom gin and dry vermouth, several dashes of orange bitters and the peel of a lemon, shaken with ice and served with an olive.

A Bradford is best mixed on the dry side, to keep its energy and intensity. Great with a zesty gin like Hayman's, Beefeater, Ki No Bi, or Death's Door with its cool blast of fennel.

MONTGOMERY

GLASS: *cocktail glass*

GARNISH: *frozen pickled silverskin onions*

METHOD: *stir with ice and strain*

15 parts gin

1 part dry vermouth

Ernest Hemingway was an assiduous Martini drinker – and a meticulous mixer of them, too. In a letter written in 1949, he specified: 'just enough vermouth to cover the bottom of the glass, ¾oz of gin and the Spanish cocktail onions very crisp and also 15 degrees below zero when they go in the glass.'

Hemingway's commitment to the perfect Martini was so great he would sometimes turn up to parties with a portable bar – a stunt that won him the friendship of socialites including the Duke and Duchess of Windsor.

His novels are awash with Martinis – most famously *A Farewell to Arms*, in which Frederic Henry, fresh from the WWI battlefield, remarks: 'I drank a couple more Martinis. I had never tasted anything so cool and clean. They made me feel civilized.' *The Garden of Eden*, Hemingway's tale of a ménage à trois, is also woozy with ice-cold gin.

His bracing 'Montgomery' formula was named for WWII Allied commander Field Marshal Bernard 'Monty' Montgomery, who would reputedly only brave battle when his troops outnumbered the enemy 15:1. **See** *p.46* for a bit more on Hemingway and his fetish for onions.

REVERSE MARTINI

GLASS: *cocktail glass*

GARNISH: *twist or olive*

METHOD: *stir with ice and strain or serve on the rocks*

50ml dry vermouth

10ml gin

1 dash orange bitters (optional)

The Reverse Martini takes the classic Dry Martini and flips it on its head, so you end up with a lighter, aperitif-style drink that is much more vermouth-led.

It's as aromatically complex as a Martini, but softer on the booze. The sort of appetite-whetting drink that's nice to have in your hand while cooking. Good on the rocks, too.

VESPER MARTINI

GLASS: *cocktail glass*

GARNISH: *lemon twist*

METHOD: *shake with ice and strain*

45ml gin

15ml vodka

and *either*

7.5ml Lillet Blanc

3 drops Angostura Bitters

or

7.5ml Cocchi Americano

The Vesper Martini was first described by James Bond in Ian Fleming's novel *Casino Royale* (1953). He instructs the casino bartender as follows:

'In a deep champagne goblet [...] Three measures of Gordon's, one of vodka, half a measure of Kina Lillet. Shake it very well until it's ice-cold, then add a large thin slice of lemon-peel. Got it?'

The Vesper has a macho reputation, but it is actually slightly sweet. The fact it's shaken rather than stirred (for more on the politics of shaken Martinis, **see** *p.66*) also helps to soften it a bit.

The French aperitif Kina Lillet was discontinued in 1986 – but you can approximate it pretty well with Lillet Blanc and a drop of Angostura Bitters (or use Cocchi Americano, a golden aperitif from Italy, which is bittered with gentian and quinine).

Bond would have probably poo-pooed modern-day Gordon's, which is bottled at a rather wimpy 37.5% abv (in the UK at least). I reckon he'd go for something with a bit more torque to it, like classic Tanqueray.

DIRTY MARTINI

GLASS: *cocktail glass*

GARNISH: *olive and five spritzes of olive brine*

METHOD: *stir with ice and strain*

50ml vodka or gin

10ml dry vermouth

10ml olive brine

The idea of ordering a Dirty Martini is fun – it feels a bit what-the-hell. But all too often the reality is a cocktail akin to pond water.

The secret is to apply the olive brine with a very light touch – definitely don't muddle olives into the drink. I like to add a bit of brine at the stirring stage and then finish with a few extra spritzes from an atomiser, so that appetising saltiness is the first thing you taste on the tip of your tongue when you take a sip.

Olives and potatoes are a great match in the kitchen – and they are in a Dirty Martini. Try using one of the full-bodied potato vodkas like Portobello Road or Luksusowa.

DUKES' (OR DIRECT) MARTINI

GLASS: *cocktail glass*

GARNISH: *Amalfi lemon twist*

METHOD: *using a dropper or dasher, put a few drops of vermouth into the frozen cocktail glass and roll it round to coat the interior. Tip away any excess. Pour the frozen spirit into the glass.*

120ml frozen gin or vodka

few drops Sacred English Dry Vermouth

Every Martini lover, at least once in their life, has to have a Martini at Dukes in St James's – the exclusive hotel bar famously favoured by Martini fiends including Martin Amis and *James Bond* author Ian Fleming.

Its reputation is formidable, but the bar itself is rather quaint – a tiny parlour-sized space muffled in thick carpets and royal-blue velvet upholstery. It's staffed by a bustling team of white-jacketed Italians, headed up by the affable Alessandro Palazzi – an avuncular chap who is equally at home discussing geopolitics or the latest Gorillaz album.

It was Palazzi's predecessor, Salvatore Calabrese (*p.163*), who invented Dukes' signature 'direct' serve, for a regular guest who complained he could never have his Martini dry enough. The Martini is prepared table-side, from a trolley, with as much flamboyance as the cramped space will allow, with spirits frozen to -22°C, a few drops of bespoke Sacred English Dry Vermouth (*p.36*), and lemons from Amalfi.

The spirit is poured straight from the bottle to frozen glass, without seeing any ice at all, so the result is silky, dense, delicious – and murderously strong.

Each Martini contains almost five whole shots of neat liquor – so pay heed to Dukes' (still very generous) two-Martini limit.

MARTINI ON THE ROCKS

GLASS: *rocks*

GARNISH: *olive/twist/pickled onion*

METHOD: *stir with ice and serve over ice*

50ml gin

25ml dry vermouth

1 dash orange bitters

A Martini on the rocks is a much more spontaneous drink than a Martini served 'up'. It's one thrown together in the heat of the moment, rather than crafted in cold blood.

It's a drink well-suited to big, bold spirits because it is a bit more dilute. And it's a forgiving formula – you don't need to worry too much about accurate measuring.

The Martini on the Rocks became fashionable in America in the 1950s – the same decade that saw the popularisation of the domestic ice-maker. It remained a bona-fide bar-call throughout the 1960s and '70s. Even so, there are many Martini fans who consider it heresy.

In *Martini, Straight Up*, Lowell Edmunds decries the Martini on the Rocks as 'an abomination' on a par with 'fast foods, rock and roll, snowmobiles, acid rain, polyester fabrics, supermarket tomatoes and books printed on toilet paper.' Its popularity in the 1960s, he said, marked the dawn of a less civilised age character-ised by 'riots, assassinations and war.' Which is quite a lot to pin on a Martini served with a bit of frozen water.

FITTY-FITTY MARTINI
BY AUDREY SAUNDERS

GLASS: *cocktail glass*

GARNISH: *lemon twist*

METHOD: *stir with ice and strain*

45ml Tanqueray gin

45ml Noilly Prat Dry vermouth

1 dash orange bitters

This modern classic by American mixologist Audrey Saunders is a nod to the vermouth-heavy Martinis of yesteryear. She launched it in 2005, at a time when the ultra-dry Martini was at its peak of popularity – I think it's fair to say this one drink had a lot to do with the ensuing vermouth renaissance.

The equal-parts ratio has the strange effect of amplifying the flavours of everything, yet it's more easy-drinking than a regular Dry Martini. Saunders recommends drinking it with food and especially fish.

The carafe in the picture was designed by Saunders for Cocktail Kingdom (**see** *Retailers – p.172*), so you can savour your Fitty-Fitty Martini sip by well-chilled sip.

FREEZER MARTINI

METHOD: *Combine the ingredients in a jug then pour into a clean 70cl bottle. Store in the freezer. Check half an hour before serving in case it needs to thaw a little.*

Makes 1 x 70cl bottle of Freezer Martini – serves about 7

For a bold gin:
430ml gin
100ml dry vermouth
170ml filtered water or bottled spring water

For a vodka or lighter gin:
450ml vodka or lighter gin
110ml dry vermouth
170ml filtered water or bottled spring water

A sense of ceremony is all well and good – but sometimes you need a Martini IMMEDIATELY. Which is why it's worth mastering the art of the ready-made Freezer Martini.

A Freezer Martini isn't just pre-mixed, it's also perfectly dilute, so you can pour it straight from frozen bottle to glass without shaking or stirring it with ice first.

It does away with the need for bar tools and ice. And because it's stored in the freezer, it keeps almost indefinitely. So you can knock up a few and keep them on standby for impromptu parties or to give as presents.

The excellent Hawksmoor group of restaurants shifts over 1,000 Martinis a month. The Freezer Martini spec included here is from Liam Davy, its head of bars.

'We would normally go for around 20–25% dilution, as a rule of thumb,' he says. 'Vodka or a lighter abv gin would be more like 20% dilution, while a big bold gin like Hepple or Tanqueray No. 10 would be more like 25%.'

'A lot of domestic freezers that don't get opened very often will freeze any diluted spirit within three to four hours,' he adds, 'so it might be worth checking on your mix half an hour before you serve it to make sure it isn't completely solid!'

For more on freezing spirits *see p.20.*

MARTINI & TONIC

GLASS: *highball*

GARNISH: *citrus slice and/or olive*

METHOD: *build over ice*

50ml gin

10ml dry vermouth

2 dashes orange bitters (optional)

Tonic water, to top up

The G&T meets the Martini in one crisp and refreshing high-ball. Be sure to use masses of ice and tonic water that's nice and cold.

VODKATINI

GLASS: *cocktail glass*

GARNISH: *olive or twist*

METHOD: *stir with ice and strain*

50ml vodka
5ml dry vermouth

Many consider the Vodkatini sacrilege – or at least very inauthentic. But vodka-based Martinis have been around since at least the 1930s.

For a brief period in the 1940s, the Vodkatini was known as the 'Kangaroo Kicker' – a name conferred on it by an American bartender in a bid to recognise the Australian allies' efforts in WWII. The name didn't stick – but if you want to test your bartender's knowledge, try ordering a 'Kangaroo'.

SEE-THRU MARTINI

GLASS: *cocktail glass*

GARNISH: *olive or twist*

METHOD: *stir with ice and strain or serve*

50ml gin or vodka

'Perfection is achieved, not when there is nothing more to add, but when there is nothing left to take away' – so said the French author Antoine de Saint-Exupéry (more or less). Is that true when it comes to the Martini? I'll let you be the judge of that.

VINTAGE

This chapter begins with the Martini's beginnings in the 1880s and runs right
through to the mid-20th century. A lot of the early recipes feature a sweet
component such as Old Tom gin, red vermouth or liqueurs. But over time you
start to see a simpler, drier-style drink emerge.

MARTINEZ

GLASS: *cocktail glass*

GARNISH: *twist and/or olive*

METHOD: *stir with ice and strain*

50ml Old Tom gin

50ml red vermouth

1 dash Angostura Bitters

Or if you don't have Old Tom:

40ml dry gin

25ml red vermouth

5ml Luxardo Maraschino Liqueur

1 dash Angostura Bitters

The Martinez is the missing link between the Manhattan and the
Dry Martini – it's got all the spicy sweetness of an old-style whis-
key drink, but you can also see the Martini's gin-and-vermouth
formula waiting in the wings.

Its heyday was the 1880s – an age when gin cocktails were
still generally made with sweetened Old Tom gin. If you want
to make an authentic Martinez, then Hayman's Old Tom is
excellent. But you can busk something good with modern-day
London Dry gin and a dash of maraschino liqueur.

You will note it's made with red, rather than dry, vermouth
– something true of many of the recipes in the Martini's
primordial soup.

It's often claimed the Martinez was created in Martinez,
California for a thirsty gold prospector. This theory has been
debunked, alas – but why let the facts get in the way of
a good story?

MARGUERITE

GLASS: *cocktail glass*

GARNISH: *orange twist*

METHOD: *stir with ice and strain*

50ml gin

50ml dry vermouth

5 drops orange curaçao or
triple sec

1 dash orange bitters

This delicate, citrusy aperitif is another early cousin of the Martini. A good choice for the gin would be Plymouth, both stylistically and historically. The dash of brandy-based curaçao orange liqueur (or triple sec, at a pinch) is there to season rather than sweeten – it warms the drink from within, like a glowing lightbulb filament.

TUXEDO

GLASS: *cocktail glass*

GARNISH: *lemon twist, discarded*

METHOD: *stir with ice and strain*

25ml dry gin or Old Tom

20ml dry vermouth

20ml fino sherry

2.5ml Luxardo Maraschino Liqueur

6 drops absinthe

2 dashes orange bitters

The Tuxedo cocktail was created in the 1890s at the same New York country club that gave the Tuxedo jacket its name. There are many variations on the theme – this one is my favourite. If you make it with dry gin, it has a tangy complexity a bit like a dry white wine. If you make it with Old Tom, it acquires a body and perfume closer to an off-dry Riesling.

FORD COCKTAIL

GLASS: *cocktail glass*

GARNISH: *orange twist*

METHOD: *stir with ice and strain*

40ml Old Tom gin

40ml dry vermouth

2.5ml Bénédictine DOM liqueur

2 dashes orange bitters

This golden Martini-style drink is an adaptation of a recipe that first appeared in *Modern American Drinks* by George J Kappeler in 1895. It skews sweet, but it's also quite aromatic and spicy – the Bénédictine gives it extravagant tobacco and incense notes. Go for Noilly Prat Dry vermouth and a nice zesty twist to see off any syrupiness.

PERFECT MARTINI

GLASS: *cocktail glass*

GARNISH: *olive*

METHOD: *stir with ice and strain*

25ml gin

25ml dry vermouth

25ml red vermouth

A Perfect Martini, like a Perfect Manhattan, is made with equal parts red and dry vermouth – but try as I might I don't find it all that good. Still, you'll find it in all the seminal cocktail books, under the name Perfect or Medium Martini. I think a slightly drier 2:1:1 formula is an improvement.

HANKY PANKY
BY ADA COLEMAN

GLASS: *cocktail glass*

GARNISH: *orange twist*

METHOD: *stir with ice and strain*

45ml gin

45ml red vermouth

2.5ml Fernet-Branca

Ada 'Coley' Coleman was head bartender at The Savoy's American Bar in the early 1900s – and she was a bit of a celebrity in her day. She created this bittersweet recipe for the actor Sir Charles Hawtrey (not to be confused with the Charles Hawtrey of *Carry On* fame). Hawtrey declared it 'the real hanky panky' – an expression that had magical, rather than sexual connotations back then – and the name stuck. Think of it as a Sweet Martini with a mean streak.

VELOCITY COCKTAIL

GLASS: *cocktail glass*

GARNISH: *orange twist*

METHOD: *shake with ice and double strain*

25ml gin
50ml red vermouth
1 orange wheel

This *Savoy Cocktail Book* recipe stretches the definition of a Martini to the limit – it would probably be more accurate to describe it as a hybrid of a Negroni, a Sangria and a Gin & It. But it's utterly delicious. So I'm going to exercise my authorial right to include it.

TURF COCKTAIL

GLASS: *cocktail glass*

GARNISH: *olive*

METHOD: *stir with ice and strain*

40ml gin

40ml dry vermouth

3 dashes orange bitters

2.5ml Luxardo Maraschino Liqueur

1.25ml absinthe

There are so many dots and dashes in this cocktail it's almost like a pointillist painting – its intricate layers of flavours are from another time and place. It's adapted from the Turf Cocktail which appears in the 1900 edition of Harry Johnson's *Bartenders' Manual*, and is named after the turn-of-the-century 'turf clubs' where New York men went to drink and gamble.

MARTINI SPECIAL

GLASS: *cocktail glass*

GARNISH: *orange twist*

METHOD: *stir with ice and strain*

50ml Old Tom gin

20ml red vermouth

1.25ml orange flower water

1.25ml absinthe

1 drop Angostura Bitters

This *Savoy Cocktail Book* Martini is a rainbow of flavour: spicy, floral, fruity, sweet. Go easy on the orange flower water as its perfume can quickly dominate everything.

ARNAUD MARTINI

GLASS: *cocktail glass*

GARNISH: *blackberry*

METHOD: *shake with ice and strain*

25ml gin

25ml dry vermouth

25ml crème de cassis

This cassis-laced Martini was named for the early 20th-century French actress and musician Yvonne Arnaud. Think of it as super-charged Kir. Best with a really dry vermouth – and shaken, not stirred.

OBITUARY

GLASS: *cocktail glass*

GARNISH: *black olives*

METHOD: *stir with ice and strain*

50ml gin

25ml dry vermouth

8 drops absinthe

This absinthe-rinsed Martini hails from New Orleans – one of the most rackety, romantic cities I've ever had the pleasure of drinking in. Why is it called the Obituary? I don't like to think. A skewer of salty black olives is the perfect antidote to the absinthe's piercing sweetness.

KUBLA KHAN NO.2

GLASS: *cocktail glass*

GARNISH: *none*

METHOD: *shake with ice and strain*

Gin

Vermouth

Laudanum

This warped elixir was the work of the notorious early 20th-century occultist Aleister Crowley. As the 'Queen of Bohemia' Nina Hamnett recalls in her 1932 memoir *Laughing Torso*: 'Crowley said he had invented a beautiful cocktail called Kubla Khan no.2 [...] He opened the cupboard and took out a bottle of gin, a bottle of vermouth and two other bottles. The last one was a small black bottle, with an orange label on it, on which was written POISON. He poured some liquid from the large bottles, and then from the black bottle he poured a few drops and shook the mixture up. The POISON, I found out afterwards, was laudanum.'

Suffice to say, don't try this at home.

SILVER COCKTAIL

GLASS: *cocktail glass*

GARNISH: *lemon twist*

METHOD: *stir with ice and strain*

30ml gin

30ml dry vermouth

2.5ml Luxardo Maraschino Liqueur

1.25ml 2:1 sugar syrup (p.160)

2 dashes orange bitters

You'd think adding half a teaspoon of maraschino liqueur would barely be worth the bother – but its lovely almond-y perfume gradually rises up to meet you as you stir. The little dash of sugar syrup adds to the drink's satiny texture.

PURITAN

GLASS: *cocktail glass*

GARNISH: *orange twist*

METHOD: *stir with ice and strain*

50ml gin

15ml dry vermouth

10ml Yellow (or Green) Chartreuse

1 dash orange bitters

There's nothing remotely puritan about this Martini twist – it's sweet and decadent. It's properly made with Yellow Chartreuse, which gives it sweet notes of honey, aniseed and spearmint. But I also like it with Green Chartreuse, which adds a more herbal character and a slight emerald tint.

ALBERTO COCKTAIL

GLASS: *cocktail glass*

GARNISH: *orange twist, discarded*

METHOD: *stir with ice and strain*

30ml gin

30ml Cocchi Americano

30ml fino sherry

This complex, pale-gold Martini-style drink is adapted from the 1937 *Café Royal Cocktail Book* – it's an elegant marriage of golden stone-fruit sweetness, sherry salt and bitter herbs. Use an en rama (unfiltered) sherry for an Alberto with a bit more oomph.

LE GRANDI ACQUE

GLASS: *cocktail glass*

GARNISH: *communion wafer with ¼ anchovy fillet on top*

METHOD: *stir with ice and strain*

20ml grappa
20ml gin
20ml kümmel
20ml sambuca

Drinks played an important part in Italy's provocative Futurist art movement. A lot of the most iconic Campari ads from the 1920s and 1930s, as well as the cuneate Campari Soda bottle, were Futurist designs.

The Futurists had a whole repertoire of cocktails they christened polibibita, or 'multi-drinks', that tended to prioritise shock and awe over deliciousness. A classic example is the Diavolo in Tonaca Nera ('Devil in Black Habit') – a cocktail of orange juice, grappa and chocolate garnished with a hard-boiled egg yolk.

The Futurist answer to the Martini was Le Grandi Acque, or 'the great waters'. It was presented at the International Colonial Exhibition in Paris in 1931. It's so intense it's almost undrinkable – the combination of anise and caraway spirits is unbearably sweet. As Cocchi vermouth maker and Futurism aficionado Roberto Bava says, the communion wafer garnish is 'just pure terrorism'.

FLAME OF LOVE

GLASS: *cocktail glass*

GARNISH: *flamed orange twist*

METHOD: *put the sherry in the cocktail glass and swirl around to coat the inside. Flame two orange twists into the glass's interior*. Shake the vodka with ice and strain into the glass.*

5–10ml fino or manzanilla sherry

3 orange twists

50ml vodka

*To flame a twist: cut an orange twist and then a light a match and hold it a couple of inches above the glass. Pinch the twist, shiny side out, into the flame so the oils ignite.

This pyrotechnic Vodkatini was created at Hollywood hangout Chasen's for the movie star Dean Martin. Martin's pal Frank Sinatra reputedly liked it so much, he bought one for everyone in the place. Bone-dry with just a whisper of nutty sherry and sweet orange oils, it's very sophisticated. Guaranteed to convert even the most die-hard Vodkatini-hater.

LUCKY JIM
BY KINGSLEY AMIS

GLASS: *cocktail glass*

GARNISH: *thin cucumber wheel or ribbon*

METHOD: *muddle the cucumber pieces firmly in the bottom of a shaker to extract the juice. Add the other ingredients, shake with ice and double-strain.*

60ml vodka

5ml dry vermouth

4cm peeled and chopped cucumber

One of my favourite bits of drinks writing is Kingsley Amis's *Everyday Drinking* – it's funny, practical and frugal (sometimes to a fault). Amis urges readers not to waste good vodka on this cocktail recipe: 'use the cheapest you can find'. The cucumber juice, he says, gives it an appearance that's 'rather mysterious… the green wine of the Chinese emperors come to vigorous life.' It's named after his comic masterpiece *Lucky Jim*, a novel that contains one of the finest hangover descriptions ever committed to print.

CONTEMPORARY

The 21st-century Martini is a much more cosmopolitan drink –
one capable of encompassing everything from Danish heather-
smoked whisky to the flavours of the Far East.

HINOKI MARTINI
BY MASAHIRO URUSHIDO

GLASS: *shot glass or stemless martini glass nestled in a masu filled with crushed ice*

GARNISH: *lemon twist, discarded, and four spritzes of hinoki tincture from an atomiser. Finish with a kombu-brined olive, rakkyo (pickled Japanese scallion bulb), and cypress leaf*

METHOD: *stir with ice and strain*

35ml vodka

35ml gin

15ml fino sherry

7.5ml junmai daiginjo sake

5ml hinoki wood tincture*

*To make 100ml: infuse 2 tbsp of hinoki wood chips in 100ml high-strength vodka for 24 hours. Strain off the liquid and divide between a dropper bottle and an atomiser.

The contemporary Martini is heavily influenced by Japan: its ingredients, its bartending techniques, its reverence for ice, its spirit of hospitality.

This recipe is by the Japanese bartender Masahiro Urushido – owner of the kitschy Katana Kitten in New York. Part izakaya, part dive bar, Katana Kitten is a fusion of two of my favourite drinking cultures – the sort of place that will serve you a world-class Martini with a side of Japanese curry sauce-drenched fries.

Hinoki, or Japanese cypress, is a highly aromatic wood that's often used in Japanese incense (you can buy chips relatively easily online) – it infuses the Martini with evocative notes of temples, pine and eucalyptus.

In a 'salute to the sake ritual', Urushido serves this elaborate Martini in a traditional wooden masu, or sake cup. The masu in the photo is from a week I spent making sake at the Akashi-Tai brewery in Japan.

The garnish is ikebana-like in its ambitiousness – you probably won't have everything on the list. But I hope, at least, you'll be able to muster a plate of curry-sauce fries to go with it.

SMOKY MARTINI

GLASS: *cocktail glass*

GARNISH: *orange twist*

METHOD: *stir with ice and strain*

50ml gin

10ml dry vermouth

2.5–5ml smoky whisky

I originally made this Martini with the Islay malt Lagavulin 16 Year Old, which has a sweet-and-savoury peatiness like lapsang souchong tea. But it's a great prism for the growing number of whiskies around the world that are smoked with more unusual things. The Arizona-born malt Del Bac Dorado is smoked with desert mesquite wood; New Zealand's Thomson distillery uses manuka; Mackmyra's Svensk Rök gets its incense-y note from Swedish juniper, while Stauning in Denmark smokes its malt with local heather. Each one of these would bring a different accent to the drink.

ALPINE VESPER
BY MIKE SAGER

GLASS: *cocktail glass*

GARNISH: *olive*

METHOD: *stir with ice and strain*

25ml Konik's Tail vodka

25ml Noilly Prat Dry vermouth

25ml Luxardo Bianco Bitter

1 dash Braulio Amaro Alpino

Equal Parts is a brilliant little Hackney bar with a very simple cocktail philosophy: all the drinks on the menu are, yes you guessed it, equal-parts-everything. This Martini tastes like a minty Negroni, but as it's made with Luxardo Bianco rather than Campari, it's nigh-on clear. If you can't get Luxardo Bianco, you can make it with Campari (though it will then, of course, be red).

HIGH FIVE MARTINI
BY HIDETSUGU UENO

GLASS: *cocktail glass*

GARNISH: *olive and lemon twist, discarded*

METHOD: *spritz the ice in the mixing glass with the vermouth, and strain off any excess. Add the gin, stir with ice and strain*

Few spritzes Martini Bianco from an atomiser

55ml frozen gin

A splash gin at room temperature

Cocktail pilgrims come from far and wide to drink at High Five, Hidetsugu Ueno's atmospheric speakeasy in Ginza, Tokyo. There's something about this basement bar – a quiet magic – that makes you forget the outside world.

Ueno-san's big quiff and braces give him a playful demeanour – but his approach to cocktails is ultra-precise. Every last detail is considered from the type of glass and the style of shaker to the size of the crystal-clear ice.

This Martini is characteristic of that meticulousness, with its whisper of white vermouth. The splash of room temperature gin is there 'to open the frozen gin up and add a bit of sweetness.'

GIN BLOSSOM
BY JULIE REINER

GLASS: *cocktail glass*

GARNISH: *lemon twist*

METHOD: *stir with ice and strain*

40ml gin

20ml white vermouth

15ml apricot eau-de-vie

2 dashes orange bitters

An antidote to the macho Martini by one of the queens of the New York bar scene, Julie Reiner. A good eau-de-vie elevates it – I love Capreolus. One of the more elegant gins, such as Plymouth or The Botanist, would also be great here.

LEFT BANK MARTINI
ADAPTED FROM A RECIPE BY SIMON DIFFORD

GLASS: *cocktail glass*

GARNISH: *lime or lemon twist*

METHOD: *shake with ice and strain*

50ml gin

15ml dry white wine

10ml dry vermouth

5ml elderflower liqueur

This elegant, elderflower-laced Martini is one for a summer's evening. It'll work with any dry, unoaked white wine: Sauvignon Blanc, Chenin Blanc or Pinot Grigio. If you don't have elder-flower liqueur, you could substitute with a slightly larger measure of elderflower cordial.

NORDIC MARTINI

GLASS: *cocktail glass*

GARNISH: *lemon twist, discarded, and either a frond of dill, a cucumber ribbon or a pickle*

METHOD: *stir with ice and strain*

50ml gin

20ml aquavit

10ml dry vermouth

Cool and clean with herbal notes of dill, caraway and fennel, this is the Martini at its most glacial. In *Everyday Drinking* Kingsley Amis describes a similar drink called 'The Copenhagen' which is garnished with a blanched almond: 'Wondering what the almond is doing there (I believe it is a Scandinavian good-luck token) will keep your guests' tongues wagging until the liquor sets them wagging about anything under the sun.'

HOGWEED MARTINI
BY MARCIS DZELZAINIS

GLASS: *cocktail glass*

GARNISH: *cucumber ribbon*

METHOD: *stir with ice and strain*

50ml gin

5–10ml white vermouth

5ml hogweed tincture*

*To make 100ml: infuse one large handful of dried hogweed seeds in 100ml vodka for 24 hours. Strain and bottle. Will keep indefinitely.

I tasted this Martini for the first time on a pebbly beach in Dorset, after a day spent foraging with bartender Marcis Dzelzainis and his portable copper still. The hogweed tincture is a kind of Anglicised version of Angostura Orange Bitters – it tastes of citrusy coriander seed and thick-cut marmalade.

Harvest the firework-shaped hogweed seed heads in late summer/ early autumn when they have dried (and make sure you've got the regular sort, not giant hogweed, which, along with some other lookalikes, is toxic).

SUIT & TIE
ADAPTED FROM A RECIPE BY KRISTINA MAGRO

GLASS: *cocktail glass*

GARNISH: *lychee*

METHOD: *stir with ice and strain*

45ml gin

20ml dry sherry

20ml Giffard Lichi-li liqueur

1 dash absinthe

A classy cross between a vintage Tuxedo (*p.101*) and a '90s Lychee Martini (*p.165*) that's as pale-pink and dry as a Provençal rosé. Magro recommends using the lychee liqueur Giffard Lichi-li, which I heartily endorse – it is hedonistically fruity and floral, yet still quite delicate.

TOMATO LEAF MARTINI

GLASS: *cocktail glass*

GARNISH: *tomato leaf and/or cherry tomato*

METHOD: *stir with ice and strain*

50ml tomato leaf-infused gin*
10ml dry vermouth

*To make 50ml: tear up a handful of tomato leaves and leave to infuse in 50ml gin for 10 minutes before straining off.

I adore the smell of tomato leaves – and their sappy green, spicy notes work brilliantly in a Martini. Pick them at the last possible moment, on a summer's evening, to capture the best of the scent.

MISTELLE MARTINI
BY RYAN CHETIYAWARDANA

GLASS: *cocktail glass*

GARNISH: *miniature pickled carrot or twist*

METHOD: *add all the ingredients to a mixing glass and leave to infuse for one minute. Add ice, stir and fine-strain (to get the seeds out)*

55ml Beefeater gin

25ml Pineau de Charentes

1 pinch caraway seeds

3 dashes orange bitters

This off-dry Martini is by Ryan Chetiyawardana – the founder of the trail-blazing Mr Lyan bar empire. 'The idea is to be able to have something a little bit more wintery, but that still drinks like a Martini,' he says. If you don't have the French aperitif Pineau de Charentes, it also works with a wine-based aperitif, such as Lillet Blanc, Cocchi Americano or amber vermouth.

TAYER'S ONE SIP MARTINI
BY MONICA BERG & ALEX KRATENA

GLASS: *shot glass*

GARNISH: *blue cheese-stuffed Gordal olive*

METHOD: *stir with ice and strain*

35ml wheat vodka

15ml Martini Ambrato vermouth

5ml Una Palma fino sherry

The London cocktail bar Tayēr + Elementary has influenced bartenders the world over with its high-low mix of culinary technique and urban cool. This Martini is one of its signatures – its bite-size proportions make it equally good as a palate sharpener or a late-night one-for-the-road. Just make sure that the shot glass is icy, icy cold.

CORONATION COCKTAIL
BY BRIAN SILVA

GLASS: *cocktail glass*

GARNISH: *lemon twist, discarded*

METHOD: *stir with ice and strain*

50ml Tanqueray or Sipsmith gin

20ml Cocchi Extra Dry vermouth

5ml Luxardo Maraschino Liqueur

I know I'm in safe hands with Brian Silva – the gravel-voiced Bostonian is a bartender very much of the old-school. He created this lovely drink for London's oldest restaurant, Rules, to mark King Charles III's coronation. Its fusion of citrus notes, juniper spice and maraschino perfume is so fresh it's almost cologne-like. Splash it all over.

FORAGED MARTINI
BY MAX AND NOEL VENNING

GLASS: *cocktail glass*

GARNISH: *lemon twist, discarded and small sprig of baby's breath*

METHOD: *stir with ice and strain*

50ml Beefeater gin

10ml Vault Coastal Vermouth

5ml Thorncroft Nettle Cordial

The fraternal founders of the stylish London bar Three Sheets have a way of making things look effortless – yet there's always so much attention to detail being paid behind the scenes. This hybrid of a Gimlet and a Martini captures that elegant under-statement perfectly, marrying English oyster shell vermouth and leafy nettle cordial with a classic London Dry gin. Stir for a few seconds longer than usual just to temper the sweetness.

TEQUILA MARTINI

GLASS: *cocktail glass*

GARNISH: *lime or grapefruit twist*

METHOD: *stir with ice and strain*

50ml blanco tequila
20ml white or dry vermouth

Really good tequila deserves to be sipped and savoured, rather than shot – and this recipe shows off the spirit at its most immaculate. Go for a proper 100% Weber Blue Agave tequila (it should say on the label), so you can taste the agave – a curiously delicious combination of lime, grilled pineapple and wet pavements. Ocho and Mijenta are great for cocktails. If money's no object, Casa Dragones Joven is also stellar.

TRUFFLE MARTINI
BY ALESSANDRO PALAZZI

GLASS: *cocktail glass*

GARNISH: *truffle cheese-stuffed olive*

METHOD: *roll the vermouth around in the glass so it coats the interior and then tip any excess away. Pour the frozen vodkas direct into the glass,*

60ml frozen potato vodka
40ml frozen truffle-infused vodka*
Few drops of dry vermouth

To make 70cl: infuse a 5g piece of Alba white truffle in a 70cl bottle of vodka (a purer-style one is best) for one month. Store in the freezer – with the truffle still in – to preserve the aromas.

This decadent Martini appears on Dukes' menu every year around mid-November, by which time the Italian truffle season is in full swing. Palazzi uses precious white truffles from Alba: 'They are expensive but the aromas are incredible,' he says. 'The drink is rich and savoury without being heavy.' A potato vodka such as Chopin would add the requisite creaminess.

SEASONED MARTINI
BY JOE SCHOFIELD

GLASS: *cocktail glass*

GARNISH: *few drops of high-grade extra-virgin olive oil*

METHOD: *stir with ice and strain*

60ml gin

5ml dry vermouth

10ml 'seasoned' fino sherry*

To make 100ml: combine 100ml fino sherry, ½ tsp salt and 1 tsp of peppercorns in a jam jar or Kilner jar. Seal, give it a shake and leave to infuse for six hours. Strain the sherry and use within 48 hours.

I gave a very entertaining talk on the Martini once with Joe Schofield, co-founder of the multi-award-winning Schofield's Bar in Manchester – and this was the Martini he served the audience. Savoury and super-dry with a delicate pepperiness, it's a fine example of the new generation of Martinis that have a more culinary influence.

TROMPE L'OEIL MARTINI

GLASS: *cocktail glass*

GARNISH: *none*

METHOD: *stir with ice and strain*

50ml vodka

2.5ml De Kuyper Dutch Cacao Crème de Cacao liqueur

1 dash orange bitters

This looks like a Dry Martini, because it's made with De Kuyper's crystal-clear Dutch Cacao liqueur, but it tastes like a cross between a Terry's Chocolate Orange and a White Russian. For a bit of fun, serve garnish-free, so the drinker has no idea what they are getting.

DIMA'S DIRTY MARTINI
BY DIMA DEINEGA

GLASS: *cocktail glass*

GARNISH: *orange or lemon twist and a side of pickles*

METHOD: *stir with ice and strain*

50ml Dima's Vodka

10ml dry vermouth

15ml beetroot pickling vinegar

'In Ukraine it is almost illegal not to have a plate of pickles accompanying your vodka,' says Dima's Vodka founder Dima Deinega. Hence the creation of this garnet-coloured twist on the classic Dirty Martini. Budmo! – or cheers! – as they say in Ukraine.

LATIN MARTINI
BY IAN BURRELL

GLASS: *cocktail glass*

GARNISH: *orange twist, discarded*

METHOD: *stir with ice and strain*

45ml Latin-style white rum

15ml Lillet Blanc, Cocchi Americano or dry/white vermouth

White rum's fine bones are beautifully showcased in this Martini by rum expert Ian Burrell. He recommends using Latin-style white rum, which tends to be lighter and more delicately fruity: Flor de Caña 4yo or Ron de Santiago de Cuba Carta Blanca, ideally – otherwise Bacardi Carta Blanca. Lillet Blanc/Cocchi Americano gives it a sun-kissed sweetness. Mancino Secco vermouth adds depth and roundness, and a little touch of spice.

BAO-TINI
ADAPTED FROM A RECIPE BY BAO

GLASS: *cocktail glass*

GARNISH: *pickled radish*

METHOD: *stir with ice and strain*

50ml Haku vodka

5ml Cocchi Dry vermouth

2.5-5ml radish pickling liquor*

To make 200g pickled radishes: clean and trim 200g of long, red radishes and combine in a Kilner jar with 65ml Chinese red vinegar, 25g caster sugar, 5g salt and half a long red chilli, de-seeded. Leave to infuse for at least 24 hours before using. Store in the fridge.

I discovered this spine-tingling Vodkatini at London's popular Taiwanese diner BAO. You must use Chinese red vinegar for the pickle, to get that far-eastern sweet-and-spicy flavour. The pickled radish garnish adds an electric-pink pop and a flare of rootsy fire.

SHISO MARTINI

GLASS: *cocktail glass*

GARNISH: *shiso leaf and/or Japanese pickled ginger*

METHOD: *stir with ice and strain*

50ml shiso-infused gin*
10ml dry vermouth

*To make 50ml: tear up one large shiso leaf and leave to infuse in 50ml of gin for 10 minutes before straining off.

I make this drink with red shiso, which I grow every year – it gives the Martini a light purple tint and the scent of wet bluebells, spicy cumin, coriander and spearmint. Excellent with Cocchi Dry vermouth, which is crunchy and green. Also good with Japanese snacks – especially sashimi.

LE SYNDICAT MARTINI

BY LE SYNDICAT

GLASS: *cocktail glass*

GARNISH: *lemon twist, discarded, and apple slice*

METHOD: *stir with ice and strain*

50ml French gin (e.g. Citadelle)
10ml Dolin Dry vermouth
10ml Boulard Grand Solage Calvados

One of my favourite bars in the world is the rackety little Le Syndicat bar in Paris. Everything from the spirits on the back bar to the hip-hop on the speakers is proudly French. This Francophile twist on a classic Martini has subtle apple and dry spice notes, as if it had been kissed on both cheeks by a tarte Tatin.

JASMINE TEA MARTINI

GLASS: *cocktail glass or tiny tea cup*

GARNISH: *lemon twist*

METHOD: *stir with ice and strain*

50ml jasmine tea-infused vodka*
10ml dry or white vermouth

To make 50ml: infuse five jasmine tea pearls in 50ml gin or vodka for 15 minutes before straining off.

Jasmine tea brings a fabulous fragrance and a subtle green-tea astringency to this elegant Martini – I like it best with a polished vodka such as Belvedere or Haku (but it could also work with a gentler gin) and one of the fresher dry vermouths such as Martini Extra Dry. A really good loose leaf jasmine tea makes all the difference: Rare Tea Co, Postcard Teas and Jing are all excellent.

TINI-TEN UMAMI MARTINI
BY PIPPA GUY

GLASS: *cocktail glass*

GARNISH: *cherry tomato*

METHOD: *stir with ice and strain*

30ml Tanqueray No. Ten gin

10ml pressed cherry tomato juice*

5ml dry vermouth

2 drops sesame oil

To make 10ml: crush three or four ripe cherry tomatoes in a jug and strain off the juice using a fine strainer.

This blush-coloured Martini may be mini, but it's an absolute flavour bomb. The fruity, umami notes of cherry tomatoes pop in combination with the zesty Tanqueray No. Ten gin. Small but perfectly formed – like a liquid canapé.

OLIO MARTINI
ADAPTED FROM A RECIPE BY JASON PATRICK GLYNN

GLASS: *cocktail glass*

GARNISH: *lemon twist, discarded, and a dot of olive oil*

METHOD: *stir with ice and strain*

50ml olive oil-washed gin*

5ml strong, cold green tea (e.g. sencha)

2.5ml dry vermouth

To make 500ml: blend 500ml of gin and 100ml of olive oil thoroughly and then freeze until the oil has set in a layer on the top. Crack the surface, strain the gin off and bottle.

Putting olive oil in a Martini sounds like madness – but trust me on this one. It brings a grassy, fruity piquancy, as well as a silky texture, to this drink. It's got to be really good olive oil though – single-estate, extra virgin and ideally recently pressed. I like to make this recipe at the end of the year when the emerald new-season olive oils are just coming in.

SPRING FORWARD MARTINI
BY SASHA PETRASKE

GLASS: *cocktail glass*

GARNISH: *trimmed ramp/ spring onion*

METHOD: *combine the gin, vermouth and the ramp/spring onion in a mixing glass and muddle gently (over-muddling will result in a bitter flavour). Add ice, stir and strain.*

60ml gin

30ml dry vermouth

1 spring onion or ramp, trimmed

This recipe was created by Milk & Honey's late founder Sasha Petraske for the now-shuttered John Dory Oyster Bar in Manhattan. 'He only wanted to be paid in oysters, which meant we had to work our way through about 100 oysters a week!' recalls his wife Georgette Moger-Petraske. 'We would drink this Martini while reading, with knees touching, and slurping our oysters.' Ramps, which are a bit like spring onions, give it a grassy freshness and a subtle, savoury pungency.

HONORARY

Love 'em or hate 'em, these recipes have been an important part of Martini's story – even if the only thing remotely 'Martini' about them is the fact they have Martini in the name.

ESPRESSO MARTINI
BY DICK BRADSELL

GLASS: *cocktail glass*

GARNISH: *three coffee beans*

METHOD: *shake very hard with ice and strain*

The original version:

50ml vodka

15ml Kahlua

10ml Tia Maria

5ml 2:1 sugar syrup (p.160)

25ml very strong, very hot espresso

My adaptation:

30ml vodka

30ml Mr Black Coffee Liqueur

15ml golden or dark rum

5ml 2:1 sugar syrup (optional)

30ml very strong, very hot espresso

The British bartender Dick Bradsell famously claimed he created this 1980s classic for a supermodel who demanded something 'to wake me up and then fuck me up.' He never disclosed, however, who that model was.

I had the pleasure of propping up Bradsell's bars around Soho on several occasions. After he died, I was given the job of writing up the Espresso Martini for the inaugural *Oxford Companion To Spirits & Cocktails*.

The recipe was originally called the Vodka Espresso – it was much simpler, then, and served on the rocks. Bradsell then re-christened it the Pharmaceutical Stimulant for the menu at Damien Hirst's Pharmacy restaurant. By the time it had become known as the Espresso Martini it had evolved into a cocktail served 'up'.

The secret is to use coffee that's really strong and hot, and to shake really hard, with lots of ice, to froth it up. 'I also like to add a pinch of salt,' says Bradsell's bartender daughter, Bea, 'it brings the drink to life.'

PASSION FRUIT MARTINI

GLASS: *cocktail glass*

GARNISH: *optional shot glass of champagne on the side*

METHOD: *shake with ice and strain*

50ml vanilla or plain vodka

15ml lime juice

15ml passion fruit liqueur (e.g. Giffard)

7.5ml 2:1 sugar syrup (see below)

Flesh of 1 passion fruit

2:1 SUGAR SYRUP

Makes 200ml

200g white caster (superfine) sugar

100ml water

Heat the sugar and water in a saucepan over a moderate heat until the sugar is completely dissolved. Leave to cool and bottle. Store in the fridge.

If you make this fruity recipe with vanilla vodka and serve it with a shot of champagne on the side, it becomes (a slightly simplified) version of Douglas Ankrah's notorious Porn Star Martini – a hedonistic 1990s classic that remains a bestseller worldwide.

EARL GREY MARTINI
BY AUDREY SAUNDERS

GLASS: *cocktail glass*

GARNISH: *wet the rim of the glass half the way round with a wedge of lemon and then dip it in caster sugar to create a rim like you get on a Margarita. Finish with a lemon twist*

METHOD: *dry-shake all ingredients without ice initially to fluff up the egg white, and then add ice, shake and strain*

45ml Earl Grey-infused Tanqueray gin*

22.5ml lemon juice

15ml 2:1 sugar syrup (p.160)

1 small egg white

*To make 45ml: combine 1 tsp good-quality loose-leaf Earl Grey with 50ml Tanqueray gin and leave to infuse for two hours (any more and it will get too tannic). Strain off the tea leaves.

This sour-style drink draws inspiration from the English ritual of afternoon tea – Audrey Saunders launched it at London's Ritz hotel in 2003. She says it was her ironic take on the fruit-tini trend of the time, but it still has great dignity, the Earl Grey bringing an aromatic, slightly tannic edge to the drink's fluffy sweet-and-sourness.

BREAKFAST MARTINI
BY SALVATORE CALABRESE

GLASS: *cocktail glass*

GARNISH: *finely shredded orange zest*

METHOD: *put the ingredients in the shaker and stir thoroughly to dissolve the marmalade. Add ice, shake and strain*

50ml gin

15ml lemon juice

15ml Cointreau

1 heaped tsp Wilkin & Son's Tiptree 'Crystal' Orange marmalade

One morning, after a particularly late night, *el maestro* Salvatore Calabrese was feeling a little bit fragile – so his wife lovingly made him a round of toast spread with marmalade. As soon as he got to work at The Lanesborough in London he set about creating this cocktail. It actually works with all sorts of fruit jams and jellies – apricot, raspberry, crab apple – but Calabrese likes marmalade's 'bittersweet, tangy taste'. 'And I do not double-strain it,' he adds, 'because I like it with the bits left *in*.'

FRENCH MARTINI

GLASS: *cocktail glass*

GARNISH: *pineapple wedge*

METHOD: *shake with ice and strain*

50ml vodka

10ml Chambord Liqueur

40ml pineapple juice

A squeeze of lemon or lime juice (optional)

This fruity French number will stand or fall entirely on the quality of your pineapple juice – you need the sharpness to cut the sweetness of the raspberry liqueur (that's why I've added an optional squeeze of citrus). Shake really hard to get the signature frothy head.

LYCHEE MARTINI

GLASS: *cocktail glass*

GARNISH: *lychee*

METHOD: *stir with ice and strain*

50ml vodka

15ml dry vermouth

10ml Giffard Lichi-li liqueur

10ml tinned lychee juice

The Lychee Martini has a rather sickly reputation but this is wonderfully delicate – perfumed, but with a fine, dry edge. It's great with Haku rice vodka. Martini Extra Dry makes it bright and pure; Noilly Dry adds a nice hint of umami. If you like this, try the Suit and Tie (*p.130*), which has a few more bells and whistles.

INDEX

RETAILERS

SPIRITS, WINES AND LIQUEURS

---

thewhiskyexchange.com

masterofmalt.com

gerrys.uk.com

amathusdrinks.com

ICE

---

icestudio.co.uk

TOOLS AND GLASSWARE

---

urbanbar.com

diffordsguide.com

cocktailkingdom.com

nudeglass.com

lsa-international.com

muddledvintage.co.uk

johnjenkins.co.uk

abask.com

kimuraglass.com

richardbrendon.com

lagomglassware.com

ABOUT THE AUTHOR

Alice Lascelles is an award-winning journalist, author, presenter and drinks expert. She writes a popular column in the *Financial Times* covering cocktails, wine and spirits and can also often be found talking about drinks on BBC Radio 4 programmes including *The Kitchen Cabinet* and on the TV. Her definitive guide for the home bartender, *The Cocktail Edit* (2022), was named a Book of the Year by *The Times*, *Financial Times*, *The Telegraph* and *Esquire*. She is also a former winner of Fortnum & Mason's Drinks Writer of the Year. When she is not writing, Alice has a second life as a musician which has included touring with The White Stripes and releasing an album under the name Alice Gun. She lives in London with her husband and two sons.

@alicelascelles
alicelascelles.com

ACKNOWLEDGEMENTS

It was over a Martini that Sarah Lavelle, Quadrille's MD, asked me to write this book – so thank you, Sarah, for giving me licence to revel in one of my favourite cocktails.

Anyone who writes about the Martini stands on the shoulders of giants – but I owe a particular debt to the mixological works of Anistatia Miller, Jared Brown, Dave Wondrich, Simon Difford and Lowell Edmunds.

Salute to all the bartenders who gave me permission to include their recipes (or variations thereon): Alessandro Palazzi, Audrey Saunders, Liam Davy, Masahiro Urushido, Mike Sager, Hidetsugu Ueno, Julie Reiner, Simon Difford, Marcis Dzelzainis, Kristina Magro, Ryan Chetiyawardana, Monica Berg & Alex Kratena, Brian Silva, Joe Schofield, Dima Deinega, Ian Burrell, all at Bao and Le Syndicat, Pippa Guy, Jason Patrick Glynn, Sasha & Georgette Moger-Petraske, Bea Bradsell, Salvatore Calabrese, Nick Strangeway and Max & Noel Venning.

And thanks to the many other drinks folk who supported this endeavour in one way or another: Robbie Bargh, Giuliano Morandin, Simon Rowe, Ago Perrone, Giorgio Bargiani, Maura Milia, Claire Smith, Tristan Stephenson, Stu Bale, Zoe Burgess, Roberto Bava, Erik Lorincz, Dale de Groff, Dave Broom, Hannah Sharman-Cox & Siobhan Payne.

Big love to my pictorial dream team: Laura Edwards, Joss Herd, Polly Webb-Wilson, Jo Cowan and Matt Hague. And to Katy Everett for the beautiful design. Cheers to editor Sarah Thickett, copy editor Nick Funnell, proofreader Emma Bastow and indexer Hilary Bird, and all in the Quadrille marketing and publicity teams. And thank you to my agent Robert Caskie, as ever, for going out to bat for me.

Ailana, so missed at cocktail hour – you are there in every page.

Bravo Alfred and George for comprehending the importance of ice at such an early age. And darling Al: I will always prefer it 5:1, but I'm prepared to meet you half way x